PAUL SPADAFORA
FIGHTING TIL THE END

PAUL SPADAFORA: FIGHTING TILL THE END
By Chris Scarnati

Published by Creative Texts Publishers
PO Box 50
Barto, PA 19504
www.creativetexts.com

Copyright 2023 by Chris Scarnati
All rights reserved

Front Cover Photo Credit: Brandon Cercone
Design copyright 2023 Creative Texts Publishers, LLC

This book or parts thereof may not be reproduced in any form, stored in a retrieval system, or transmitted in any form by any means—electronic, mechanical, photocopy, recording, or otherwise—without prior written permission of the publisher, except as provided by United States of America copyright law. "Creative Texts" and "Creative Texts Publishers" are registered trademarks of Creative Texts Publishers, LLC. All Rights Reserved.

The accounts in this biography are true, but some names and identifying features have been changed or wholly omitted to protect the privacy of individuals.

ISBN: 978-1-64738-091-5

PAUL SPADAFORA
FIGHTING TILL THE END

**By
Chris Scarnati**

**Foreword by
Roy Jones Jr.
&
Tom Yankello**

To my son, Jacob, who fought bravely till the end.

Table of Contents

Foreword i
Chapter 1: Sin City Salvation 1
Chapter 2: Unfortunate Son 6
Chapter 3: Road From Perdition 21
Chapter 4: P.K.'s Prodigy 33
Chapter 5: Ballrooms and Boxing Gloves 43
Chapter 6: Coronation of a King 58
Chapter 7: The Fourth Franchise 97
Chapter 8: In the Confluence of Chaos 118
Chapter 9: Loaded and Dangerous 142
Chapter 10: The Second Act 155
Chapter 11: A Fallen Star 184
Chapter 12: The Last Round 197
Notes 202
Acknowledgments 215
About the Author 219

Foreword
By Roy Jones Jr. and Tom Yankello

Roy Jones Jr.

Many people in boxing have a story to tell.

I had known about Paul Spadafora and watched him from afar for a long time. Paul was one of the best defensive fighters I had ever seen. Not a lot of people could fight the style of fight he fought.

And I also knew about the drugs and alcohol.

I'm the kind of guy who will always give a person a chance to pursue their best life. That's why I wanted to take Paul on as a fighter with TNT, my old promotional company. The way I looked at it was Paul had to be pretty damn awesome to do the stuff he did in the ring and remain *undefeated* for so long with all of his issues. The man had all kinds of things going on outside the ring that should have stood in his way, but he still kept winning.

God had to be watching out for him.

We didn't get to accomplish everything we wanted to with Paul at TNT because of a few outside issues, but we did the best we could. It would have been an absolutely awesome fight if Paul had finally gotten his chance to face Floyd Mayweather Jr. in a sanctioned bout. Paul didn't have Floyd's power, but he was better defensively. The reason it would have been a great matchup is because they were both the best at what they did.

I think Paul can be a successful trainer because he's one of a kind. How many white guys do you see that have had that kind of defensive presence about them? He's very unique, and his ring IQ is really high. I'm hoping Paul can take what he has learned from his past and try to instill it into others so they won't go down the same road he did with drinking.

I also hope this book does well because Paul's story can be an important lesson to many people. He was already a great champion, but he could have done so much more.

The title of this book, *Fighting Till the End*, definitely sums up Paul because he will be fighting his entire life. There will be the fight to stay clean and sober, and there will be the fight to find a boxer he can turn into the next world champ. Vegas is where all the fighters go, so he is in an excellent place to do it.

Paul has heart. He was a hell of a fighter and remains a hell of a person.

-Roy Jones Jr.
October 2023

***

Tom Yankello

Paul once posted on my Instagram account, "Stupid-ass addiction kills lives, stops everything, and holds you back. It puts doubt and fear into your heart. When I was pure, I really believed wholeheartedly I would have been one of the greatest. But it's over. I can now try to give what I've learned to others, and when I watch you, Tommy, it never stops. You are a real teacher!" And I can say I am the one person who knows how true that statement is. Paul, without a doubt, would have been one of the greatest fighters in the history of boxing if it weren't for his addiction.

I greatly respect Paul as a fighter, and for him to recognize me like that makes me feel good. It means a lot when a guy of that caliber and ability sees me that way. At the same time, I feel a bit of regret. No matter how great a trainer someone is, they will never win the Kentucky Derby with a donkey. Paul was a talented thoroughbred in boxing – especially in Pittsburgh, where football is king. In these parts, you don't get a guy who loved boxing like he did, was dedicated to the sport like he was, or had the dream and passion of becoming a world champion as he did.

But sadly, his addictions sabotaged so much of his success. I noticed these problems from the beginning, especially with the alcohol. By the time his record was 13-0, he was twenty-one-years-old. There would be lapses when he would completely disappear on me between bouts, making me think, "Why would a guy who trained like an absolute madman in the gym suddenly disappear for four or five days with no phone call." I would start to catch wind that it was because he was at the bar all night.

Paul and I became fast friends because of our shared love of boxing. I don't think I've met anyone who loves it as much as we both do. Paul was one of the best. And without the drugs and alcohol, he would have been unstoppable. He would not have needed so many people around him; he would have had a clearer vision of what he wanted to accomplish and had more confidence.

It makes me think about the present. If Paul were to come to me at this point in my coaching career, things would have been considerably different. With him sober, I could have implemented more of myself into helping him achieve his fullest potential. I don't want to disrespect any of the guys I've trained, but Paul was my most well-rounded boxer. That means he gets an "A" in almost every category. His power was underrated by most, but I'd still give him a solid "B."

Most evidently, Paul was one of the best defensive fighters and the most cerebral the sport has ever seen. He could fight on the inside and outside and was as quick as a cat, but his mind worked more rapidly than anyone I have ever trained.

Roy Jones Jr. was also quick-minded but benefitted from being faster physically. Paul's quickness was mostly mental. His ability to process information was off the charts. Tom Brady can read a play more quickly than anyone else. He doesn't have to be as fast as many of these other quarterbacks because he's making the move in his *mind* before everyone else. Paul could always control the pace and neutralize his adversary's speed. And you couldn't just be fast with Paul because he would always be mentally ahead of you, which always allowed him to be in position to make you miss.

You hear the idiom, "People have to live and learn." Stories like Paul's, however, can educate people so they won't have to learn a hard lesson about what alcohol and drug addiction can do. People from the outside looking in might comment, "What do you mean? Paul was successful." But these people don't comprehend that Paul could have been even *more* successful. They don't understand the torture that was Paul's life. People see a record of 49-1-1 and say, "That was only one fight from being undefeated." But Paul never got the opportunity to fight other greats to prove to the world how special he truly was, and he will be the first to tell you the same. Someone once told me that the definition of Hell is when the person you are meets the person you could have become. That is hard to swallow.

I've stayed in touch with Paul since he moved from Pittsburgh to Las Vegas, and I hope he continues to move in the right direction. He really has a lot to offer as a trainer. When Paul is in the corner during a bout, he can anticipate and process both the flaws of his fighter and his fighter's opponent. He can see the mannerisms and tendencies of any boxer. He can give advice to keep his pupils safe in the ring. This ability will always set him apart.

Chris Scarnati does a great job covering the trials and tribulations of a great fighter who, sadly, should have been even greater.

-Tom Yankello
September 2023

Chapter 1: Sin City Salvation

Paul Spadafora remembers the gamut of emotions, the dizzying highs and lows, the triumphs and gut-wrenching tragedies. They visit him in daydreams and haunt him regularly in nightmares.

He does his best to suppress the memories and focus on the present. Amidst the rhythmic rat-a-tat of speed bags, swooshing of jump ropes, and the violent symphony of jabs, body shots, and haymakers being exchanged within the walls of the DLX Boxing Gym in Las Vegas, Paul can be heard barking commands at his son, Geno, a sinewy 18-year-old amateur bantamweight who flaunts his dad's shifty movement and same sneaky uppercut.

"I want to get him as many fights as we can for two years and turn him pro," Paul says. "If he does the right thing, you never know how far he could go."

Geno knows he should listen because very few have made it as far as his old man.

Paul gave Pittsburgh its first boxing title in more than 50 years after defeating Israel "Pito" Cardona to capture the International Boxing Federation (IBF) lightweight belt in 1999. He was commonly called "The Pittsburgh Kid," a tag owned initially by the late Charles "P.K." Pecora (his first trainer) and Billy Conn, the acclaimed light-heavyweight champ from the city's East Liberty section who once galvanized the nation by nearly upsetting a seemingly immortal adversary named Joe Louis.

In Paul, locals wondered whether they were witnessing Conn's second coming. Sportswriters lauded his meteoric rise, and his management team even dubbed him Pittsburgh's fourth franchise behind the Steelers, Pirates, and Penguins. "Paul represented a renaissance in (Pittsburgh) boxing – a rebirth of the tough, working-class fight town Pittsburgh originally was between the 1920s and 1950s," explained boxing historian Douglas Cavanaugh. "With Paul, it was like 'Oh my God, boxing is back!' and everyone was ready for it."

The excitement generated inside the ring was rarely instantaneous. Paul was never revered for his knockout power but dominated fights as a slick defensive southpaw conditioned to win 12-round marathons. He relied on guile, deceptive quickness, and a prodigious counterpunch, which, according to trainer Tom Yankello, was almost rooted in superhuman telepathy. "(Paul) always seemed to be a move ahead of his opponents," he told *Sports Illustrated*. "Larry Bird always had an instinct to know where the basketball was coming off the backboard. Paul was like that as a boxer – always in the right position."

This sixth sense kept him from getting hurt. "Nobody could hit Paul," said Jesse Reid, another trainer who helped coach him through his eight title defenses. "He's a special boxer who is up there with the best of them. He always brought an extra dimension."

Paul approached the sweet science with the fevered intensity of a mad scientist, and the gym was his fistic laboratory. He spent entire days sparring with multiple partners and long nights breaking down video footage to prepare for his next bout. Boxing brought out his best qualities. It defined his purpose and made him feel whole.

And when keeping him occupied, it quelled demons that would otherwise make his reality a living hell.

SIN CITY SALVATION

As detailed in the media for more than two decades, Paul's debilitating addictions between fights contributed to a criminal rap sheet that rivaled his résumé of accomplishments. He was a tortured soul, a veritable Dr. Jekyll and Mr. Hyde. His narrative was one of brilliance, crippled by madness, a dichotomy of in-ring savant and out-of-ring calamity.

Alcohol was the catalyst for every bad experience, and in its wake laid a trail of pain and incarceration. It was the reason the police inadvertently shot him.

It was the reason he accidentally put a bullet through the woman he loved.

The liquor led Paul to use hardcore drugs. Nothing was off limits, especially during the several occasions he attempted to kill himself. "If Paul would have had five years of an honest life, he would have been one of the top fighters to ever live," lamented Paul's older brother, Harry Spadafora. "God's plan for Paul was different than Paul's plan for Paul."

Paul falls into a wistful trance when reminiscing about his July 2014 unanimous decision over Hector Velazquez. The victory capped off a sterling career but left him feeling unsatisfied.

Despite his long reign at the top, Paul remains tormented by the realization he never reached his fullest potential. When left alone, his thoughts turn dark and compel him to seek solace in the bottle. "It (sobriety) is terribly hard... so hard," he says. "I constantly have the devil sitting on my shoulder telling me to blow everything off and to go have another drink."

Paul's flesh illustrates his personal history. Tattoos covering his biceps, torso, neck, and back display a mosaic of crime, family, drug abuse, fame, fortune, and heartbreak. His right forearm displays images of his children. His opposing limb showcases sketches of a crack pipe, an ecstasy pill, and a heroin needle and stamp bag, all encircling the word "Truth." In recent years, Paul extended the canvas to include "PK" (Pittsburgh Kid) and "G$" (Geno Spadafora) on each temple.

His most meditative ink, however, is preserved in a stack of journals he started as a child. Paul penned his thoughts as he tried to make sense of his strained connection with his father and its devastating outcome. The prose became a needed distraction during the unnerving period he lived with a pedophile. It provided clarity when he reflected on his mother's struggle to earn a paycheck while stumbling through abusive relationships. Later, the pages would imbue him with a sense of responsibility to stay clean so he could buy her the home he felt she deserved. "I would write to God when I was training, but then I would stop after a fight when I was drinking," he says. "But I needed it. You need somebody, some type of thing. I would write to God and tell him I was trying to do the right thing, trying to say the right things. It made me feel something, so I kept going."

Paul speaks with a childlike naivety that belies his hardened exterior. He cares about public perception and feels like he is misunderstood continuously. He is determined to learn from his mistakes and aspires to leave behind a legacy not defined by his vices and vulnerabilities.

He hopes his relocation to Vegas, the world's fight capital, was a step in the right direction. "I would like to train real fighters and get them off the street," he says proudly. "It's going to happen – you watch!"

SIN CITY SALVATION

Reid thinks Paul is already an excellent mentor to young boxers but still expresses concern. "A lot of people didn't think much of Paul in the beginning, but once he started rolling (as a boxer), people started to see that he was sensational," he says. "He had great, great skills. But when you put drugs and drinking into the mix, it just tears you up. It's sad because you love Paul and care about him so much that you just wish you could press a button and stop it all, but it doesn't work that way. You can try to talk to someone a million times to get them to change, but sometimes it just doesn't happen."

Paul realizes he must – there is no alternative. He remains upbeat in the face of cynics and is committed to fighting the good fight until the very end, just as he always did in the ring.

He leans against the ropes and nods in the affirmative while watching Geno rattle a combo against his opponent's ribs. "I'm doing what I want to do, and I'm not going to stop doing what I want to do," he says. "I want people to see my story, so maybe someone else doesn't have to go through what I've gone through. That means I'm helping someone."

After pondering his past, Paul laughs and points to the sky. "At the end of the day, I'm just trying to go up there," he adds. "I've been stressed for as long as I can remember, dawg. I just want to get up there by doing the right thing."

Chapter 2: Unfortunate Son

In a career spanning two decades and multiple titles, no fighter influenced Paul's life more than his mother.

Ann Marie Polecritti was born in Pittsburgh to Eugene and Betty Polecritti on November 20, 1950. The pregnancy was unplanned, and the marriage was unsteady. Eugene doubted his wife would ever make a suitable mother, so he sent Annie to live with her grandparents, George and Beatrice Polecritti, before she was eventually adopted by his sister and her husband, Teresa and Harold Miller of O'Hara Township.

Teresa could not conceive her own children, so the Millers raised Annie as their only child in an old farmhouse. Nevertheless, she grew up surrounded by 16 cousins she treated like close siblings. Annie followed their lead into sports and joined the cheerleading squad and girls' basketball team. She was a natural at both and reveled in the thrill of competition.

She also valued helping others, particularly in her care for Beatrice, a partially blind diabetic amputee confined to a wheelchair. They read the Bible daily and forged a tight bond steeped in a shared devotion to God. "My grandpap put me in a Catholic school, and I was taught by the nuns," she said. "I got interested in the church a whole lot, and I just wanted to become one of them. I thought I could be on my own, make a nice living, and have a place to stay."

After graduating from Ursuline Academy High School, Annie enrolled in the Sisters of Divine Providence at La Roche College in Pittsburgh. She continued along a spiritual journey she imagined would one day lead her to the convent before fate took her in a wildly unexpected direction.

Silvio Spadafore introduced himself to Annie at a dance in the early summer of 1968. Annie was smitten when their paths intertwined again at another community-sponsored event.

They spent the evening entrenched in deep conversation. Silvio asked Annie on a date, and they rushed into a passionate courtship.

Silvio was the son of Frank and Virginia Spadafore, two first-generation immigrants from Calabria, Italy. He was a star football player at Sharpsburg High School and a Pennsylvania Golden Gloves Boxing Champion at 165 pounds. Annie's earliest get-togethers with him included trips to the drive-in movie theater and late-night rendezvous at the local Eat-n-Park restaurant. She loved watching Silvio race his 1969 Chevelle 396 SuperSport at the local track. He was suave and well-mannered, but Annie was mainly drawn to the charming aspect of his broken English. Her family found him equally enchanting, with one exception. "My (adopted) father, Harold, was German and was pushing me to marry this other German kid, but there was nothing there," she said. "Harold didn't like Italians, and he certainly didn't want me to ever marry someone like Silvio."

But Annie was past caring. She had fallen so hard that she began questioning her original ambitions. Her feelings for him intensified toward the end of her first year at La Roche, initiating a daring decision that would infuriate Harold and forever alter the course of her life. "(Silvio) told his parents he was leaving for the police academy to become a state trooper, and I told mine that I was heading to a religious retreat with my Ursuline Academy (High

School) Sisters," she said. "We really left the state and ended up getting married by the Justice of the Peace in Winchester, North Carolina."

Annie and Silvio returned to Pittsburgh as newlyweds. Once both sets of parents begrudgingly came to grips with their children's out-of-state nuptial, Silvio remarried Annie at St. Mary Catholic Church in Sharpsburg. The ceremony included a wedding party of 14 and a guest list of several hundred. Annie lost herself in the pageantry and imagined the beginning of something profound and permanent.

During their first few years together, everything indeed supported this vision. Silvio found work in construction, and Annie gave birth to their first son, Harry Spadafore, on July 5, 1971. Annie planned to expand their family with more children and romanticized growing old and gray with her spouse.

Only after Annie helped land Silvio a higher-paying gig as a crane operator did she notice changes in his temperament. They were subtle at first, with Silvio spending more and more time away from home. But as weeks passed, he became distant. Annie suspected infidelity but tried to convince herself there had to be a practical explanation.

Her worst fears were confirmed the day a police officer found a package containing women's lingerie along the highway and delivered it to her apartment. The name "Alva" was scribbled across the front, along with Silvio's name on the return address.

In Annie's mind, the real writing was on the wall. "I told Silvio's mother I couldn't be with him anymore because every day I woke up and my life felt miserable," she said. "She didn't want us to break up, but when I found out he was cheating, it was over."

Silvio had been Annie's first love. He was the father of her son and the breadwinner of their small family. And now she confronted the harsh certainty of moving forward as an unemployed single mom.

Compounding her adversity, Annie learned she was pregnant.

***

Paul Ross Spadafore entered the world kicking and screaming on September 5, 1975, at St. Margaret's Hospital in Aspinwall. Though it would be 11 years before Annie's newborn would first step into a boxing ring, he arrived with an innate propensity to inflict punishment. "Harry took 16 hours, and Paul took just 11, but it was much worse with him," she said. "It was so bad that I had to wrap my legs around this heavy-set nurse as she screamed 'PUSH!' It was the worst pain of my life."

Paul rewarded his mom with good behavior. He was a quiet baby who grew into a well-balanced toddler. He carried around a Wonder Woman doll everywhere he went. He was low maintenance, happy, and needed no help finding ways to entertain himself.

Spadafore would remain on Paul's birth certificate, but his uncle (also named Paul) persuaded Annie to informally switch her family's last name to *Spadafora*, just as he had done, to make it sound more Italian.

It was also a ploy to help his former sister-in-law move forward.

With Silvio out of the picture, Annie worked several jobs tending bar and turned her attention to other suitors in a push to mend her broken heart. She had chatted with a man named Jim during her marriage but began seeing him often during her separation. She thought he was entertaining. He also held down steady employment as a laborer, so she counted her blessings.

Initially.

Jim eventually developed an addiction to drugs and alcohol. One morning, he entered her house following a long night of drinking. He slurred obscenities, became fixated on a TV set she had purchased, and looked for a blunt object he could use to smash it into pieces. When Annie intervened, Jim slammed her to the carpet and rained hammer fists onto her head.

Paul and Harry watched helplessly from the corner, too young to understand what was happening to their mom and too small to protect her. But in those horrifying minutes, they also observed Annie's inner strength when she pulled a steak knife from beneath a couch cushion and stabbed him in his side. The steel plunged through Jim's flesh repeatedly, diminishing his punches and causing him to crumple on her like a deflating parade balloon.

Paramedics carted Jim to the nearest emergency room before police took Annie to jail. As Paul later learned, the encounter lent credence to the name she earned on the streets.

Nobody would push "Crazy Annie" around.

After leaving Jim, Paul was relieved his mom moved on to dating a man named William, a wealthy owner of a thriving dump truck company. William treated Annie's children with generosity and respect. He once slipped $500 into her Bible to help pay for groceries and utilities. "He took care of us all," Annie said. "He was the only one I really should have married. We could have had a really good life together."

UNFORTUNATE SON

Safe and comfortable was nice, but Annie fell under the spell of Anthony, a patron she would often serve while working at a tavern in Etna. Anthony worked as a mechanic daily and rolled with a motorcycle gang each night. He exposed Annie to raucous parties and reckless abandon. He was ruggedly attractive and always on the prowl for adventure. "I really liked him a lot," she said, "and I really liked the wild life he showed me."

The pair moved into a house in Millvale and consummated their union when Annie gave birth to another son, Charlie, at St. Francis Hospital on April 26, 1977. Annie admitted it was the easiest of her three pregnancies. "By the time we got to the delivery room, (Charlie) pretty much dropped out," she said.

When William wed another woman, Annie walked down the aisle again and married Anthony.

It was a slapdash decision she would ultimately regret.

***

Anthony and Annie never set out to be Ozzie and Harriet. They resembled a nuclear family in appearance, but Anthony remained immersed in the nightlife, and Annie sold cocaine while bartending to make ends meet.

Their young children, meanwhile, devised inventive ways to ditch school. Paul was the most committed. When Anthony dropped him off at his bus stop each morning, Paul would sneak to the back of a nearby Shop-n-Save supermarket and hide amongst the discarded boxes in the stock room until the school day ended. He was eventually caught, but it took over a month for Annie to discover his truancy.

On another occasion, Annie overheard Paul and Charlie in the backseat of her car when they were supposed to be attending class. "They were under a pile of winter jackets," she said. "I would never have known had I not heard Paul whisper 'Move over.'"

Although they shared humorous memories, Annie's marriage to Anthony languished. The process was hastened by Annie's mother, Teresa, who never hid her disapproval of the union. Annie claimed Anthony was always resentful of Teresa's influence and fumed whenever she meddled in their affairs.

The tension reached a crescendo after Teresa was diagnosed with terminal cancer in November of 1981, and he allegedly sent a bouquet of black roses to her hospital bed with a card that read, "I want you to see this before you pass away."

Annie threw Anthony out of their home. Rather than getting in the last word, she asserted Anthony attempted to get in the last shot when he rolled up to their Millvale dwelling, aimed a 30-30 hunting rifle toward the front bay window, and pulled the trigger. The bullet pierced the glass, went through the bathroom (where Paul and Charlie happened to be taking a bath), and lodged into the kitchen wall an inch above Annie's head. "I was sitting at the table paying one of my mom's medical bills when it happened, and Harry screamed from his upstairs bedroom, 'Ma, that was a gun!'" she said. "I told him to get under his bed, dragged Paul and Charlie out of the bathtub, threw them behind the couch, and then called the cops."

When the chief of the Millvale Police Department telephoned Anthony, Annie claimed Anthony incriminated himself further when he threatened to return and burn down her house.

"The chief told him, 'We're coming for you,'" she said.

Anthony faced charges on multiple accounts and eventually served seven years in Allegheny County Prison.

Before sentencing, Silvio, who by this time had married Alva, took Paul and Harry away.

Paul climbed into his dad's Ford pickup and sat in the middle console next to Harry. During the drive, he looked in the rearview mirror and sobbed.

His thoughts drifted to his mother. She made horrible mistakes with men, and, unbeknownst to him then, the drugs she covertly peddled would eventually lead to an insufferable addiction.

Excluding these flaws, Annie personified resiliency, and Paul would often return to his earliest memories of her and find inspiration.

"If you're in a war, wouldn't you want to fight alongside a soldier that's been through some shit?" he asked. "Annie is a good person. She's a good mom. She never quits."

***

Silvio lived with Alva on a quiet street in Heidelberg, a small borough along Pittsburgh's outskirts just 12 miles away from Annie's Millvale home.

For Paul and Harry, it felt like they had traveled lightyears away to a distant planet.

Annie always worked irregular shifts at the bar. Once they ended, sloshed patrons slid off their stools and staggered to her place for after-hours bashes stretching into the early morning. Her porch generated more traffic than a Greyhound station. Strangers would pass out and nurse their hangovers on the family couch for days. There were no bedtimes or routine dinners under Annie's roof. Anarchy reigned supreme.

At Silvio's, there was security and structure. Paul and Harry attended St. Ignatius, a well-regarded Catholic school. They ate meals with the entire family (which included his stepmom's three older children). Lights flicked off on weeknights at reasonable hours, and, for a brief period, Paul relished having his own bedroom.

But deep down, the conventional comforts mattered little to Paul because he felt like an outcast with an ambiguous ancestry. Charlie belonged to Anthony, and Harry belonged to Silvio. Despite Annie's insistence that Paul was also Silvio's son, Silvio assumed differently and treated Paul as if he was Jim's child.

Paul starved for his dad's attention but found indifference.

Silvio coached Harry's youth football and basketball teams and would only attend Paul's games on rare occasions. Paul treasured those fleeting moments. He already excelled as an athlete, but they motivated him to pump his legs harder to shake an extra tackle or press with more energy to hit an extra jump shot. "I wanted to do well for (Silvio), but he didn't care that much, I guess," Paul said. "He didn't abandon me, but he always cared more for Harry, and that was obvious."

The things Silvio did behind closed doors were less evident, and they would later tie Paul to his lineage in the most tragic of ways.

***

Harry woke up on November 15, 1984, to find Silvio lying face-down on the living room carpet. He dialed 911 after several attempts to revive him proved futile. Paul, only nine, watched paramedics cart his father away on a gurney. "They (doctors) called later and said he had passed away, and that was the end of it," Harry explained. "It was a drug overdose."

The finality of Silvio's death was too surreal for Paul to digest. He wore his best shirt and tie to the funeral and stumbled around in a stupor. "Harry was crying his eyes out, but people might have looked at me and said, 'How come Paul don't look like he cares?'" Paul said. "I was almost trying to force myself to cry."

Silvio was 33 years old when he perished, but his unresolved issues with Paul remained alive. Paul perseverated over what he could have done differently to win his dad's affection. He brooded over what compelled Silvio to use drugs in the first place. The sadness Paul felt over their complex relationship kept him awake many nights.

He understood that this part of him was broken and would forever remain that way.

Paul and Harry remained with Alva and returned to St. Ignatius. They immersed themselves in their sports seasons. It was a distraction that enabled them to cope with their loss.

But after a while, sports would also be the reason their living arrangement with Alva fell apart. Paul became incensed with Alva one summer when she prohibited him from signing up for football tryouts. He pleaded to return to Annie. When the back-and-forth bickering amplified, Alva finally caved, and Annie jumped in a cab and brought Paul and Harry back to her new quarters.

Paul was thrilled, but the reunion was bittersweet. He had been pining for the unconditional love of his mom – a person who would never reject him – and was overjoyed about reconnecting with Charlie.

He also realized he was being released back into the wild.

Annie had moved to Garfield, a crime-infested neighborhood inside the city limits. The streets were unsafe. The sound of gunshots rumbled across the skyline regularly, and his family room did not feel any safer. "I didn't have to worry about strangers at Silvio's," Paul said. "When I went (to Annie's) home, I never knew what was going to happen or who was going to be there."

Paul's transition to Fort Pitt Elementary was similarly problematic. The inner-city public school was the antithesis of his parochial education in Heidelberg, and the unsupervised bathrooms and crowded fourth-grade hallways facilitated his earliest foray into fisticuffs. "I was one of maybe two or three white kids in the entire building," Paul said. "It's there where I learned I liked to fight."

Annie often switched jobs over the next two years, moving the boys to North Hills, Sheridan, Lawrenceville, and Millvale apartments. Paul transitioned in and out of various schools, and it decimated his grades. "Mostly, you wouldn't even see a report card," she said. "Paul would tell his teachers, 'I can't find my mother to get her to sign it.'"

With Annie working double shifts, Paul was usually being honest. He experienced more freedom with Annie than he ever did with Alva and savored his new independence.

But the idle periods, naturally, led him to trouble.

Paul's problems started the day he brought home a wallet filled with cash, claiming he "discovered it" tucked between some railroad ties. The following afternoon,

UNFORTUNATE SON

Annie became suspicious when Paul and Charlie accumulated an armful of Nintendo cartridges they had serendipitously "found" in the same location.

The truth surfaced the following week when two detectives interrogated Paul and Charlie in separate squad cars. Paul was identified as the ringleader and arrested. "Charlie told them every house they went to (and robbed)," Annie said. "Next thing I know, they're taking Paul to juvenile court, and Harry tells me, 'Those boys disgraced our name again.'"

Paul's criminal record did little to deter him from shoplifting an outfit at a Horne's department store a few months later. "(Police) got me right in front of the entrance," Paul said. "I'm pretty sure Harry ratted me out that day."

Recognizing a pattern, Annie decided to teach Paul a lesson he could comprehend. She sent Paul to the basement and ordered him to drop his pants before delivering several whips to his buttocks with the cord from an iron.

Paul ran from the house in tears. His mother had hurt him both physically and emotionally. He was hell-bent on getting even and made an unwise phone call from a neighbor's kitchen.

A police officer later returned with Paul and knocked on the front door. When Annie answered, the man looked down at Paul, sighed, and uttered, "You're on your own, son."

"I never trusted a cop again because, after that, she *really* beat the fuck outta me," Paul said.

Annie served as the family cook, chauffeur, and grief counselor, but her primary role was disciplinarian. No one was immune to her rule of law – not even at work. "A lady took my seat one time at the bar," Paul said. "My mom told her it was my seat, but the lady didn't care. So my mom says, 'Watch this,' puts down her drink, and beats the lights outta her."

Annie's homespun wisdom was consistently reinforced with bruises and bloodshed. Jim had been on its receiving end years earlier and was given a refresher course weeks after Annie permitted him to move into their home. Paul was astonished she could trust a louche degenerate she had once sent to the ER and hated seeing them back together as a couple.

He was *not* surprised, however, when Jim relapsed into his old habits and disappeared with several hundred dollars of her money, nor by what happened to him next.

Annie knew she would recoup most of her cash, but she also wanted to send Jim a message and paid a hulking male acquaintance to deliver it. She strapped her sons into seat belts that night and followed the hired thug to a decrepit road in The North Side, an older section of Pittsburgh hugging the northern banks of the Allegheny and Ohio Rivers.

Once their target was locked in, Annie parked a few spots away and enjoyed the show while her sons gaped in horror. "(Jim) was in a car, shooting dope, getting all fucked up," Paul said, "and then this dude pulled him out, beat the life outta him, took the rest of the money, and gave it back to my mom."

Jim was treated at a nearby hospital for a broken arm and ribs. But Paul said his ego sustained the most damage when Annie visited his bedside, looked him in the eyes, and said coldly, "This is what you do to someone who takes from your family."

***

UNFORTUNATE SON

Annie was a fierce lioness around her cubs, but she was frequently away from the den. Consequentially, the Spadafora boys often had to fend for themselves and, with little supervision, forge their own paths.

Harry's buddies called him "Spat" and Paul "Spit" (past- and present-tense plays on their last name). Aside from the similar sobriquets, they grew up quite differently. Harry adopted Annie's work ethic while watching her hustle at multiple jobs and found employment at a pizza shop by age 16.

He also developed Annie's temper, which flared around the miscreants she brought home. "I beat up a few of her boyfriends," Harry said. "I started knocking them out when I was a teenager and got bigger."

Even though they often disagreed as brothers typically do, Paul admired Harry. In addition to being his de facto father figure, he was responsible, outspoken, and, as the oldest son, Paul's first male role model.

Charlie, by contrast, was Paul's sidekick, and the bedrock of their alliance was mischief. Neighbors would spot them driving Annie's truck around town, cautioning her to take note of where she had previously parked. One Sunday, Annie observed Paul and Charlie pull a *dirty* prank on the tenant living underneath their second-floor apartment. "I saw this lady leaving with this big church hat on, and all of a sudden, I see something fly out our window and plop on her hat," she described. "She takes it off and starts freaking out. One of the boys had stuck their hand down the toilet and thrown poop onto it."

Some of their crimes were less comedic. Annie seethed the afternoon she heard they had been caught eating stolen snacks in the back of a convenience store. "(Paul and Charlie) told the clerk they were hungry because their mother never feeds them," she said. "You should have seen the beating they got that time. I made them put their hands on the table and gave it to them real good."

Annie's physicality horrified Paul but never Charlie. His little brother was a thrill-seeker who lived on the edge. Sometimes, he enjoyed jumping from one. "Charlie would climb to the top of the football fence, do a perfect backflip, and land on his feet," Paul said. "He was a great athlete, but he didn't want to take up sports. He just wanted to smoke cigarettes and started doing that when he was only 10 years old!"

Paul appreciated his brothers. He also felt like an outcast in a world that would never truly accept him.

Conscious of his limitations, he hunted for something better. In the eyes of an underprivileged pre-teen, this could only be appraised by the accumulation of material possessions his mother could not provide.

He was prepared to roll the dice and make significant adjustments to get whatever he wanted, no matter the cost.

The repercussions of these rudderless choices would remain with Paul forever.

Chapter 3: Road From Perdition

Annie moved her sons across the city to Westwood shortly after Paul turned 12. One balmy September night, he and a classmate walked to a nearby park to shoot hoops. Along the way, his friend seemed apprehensive as they passed a parked sedan. Inside was a middle-aged man – the boy's football coach – gesturing for him to sit in the passenger's seat.

The sun had just set, and the street lights cast an ominous glow over the vehicle. It was after 8 p.m., and no other adult was in sight.

Paul's buddy was too frightened to approach the driver-side window, so Paul went in his place. He was startled to see the man crying. Things turned eerie when he handed Paul four sheets of paper. Upon a cursory inspection, Paul noticed sentences that were saccharine and sentimental and quickly grasped that he was holding an intimate letter intended for his friend. Paul felt sick as he turned around to deliver the note, realizing it came from an adult who should not be around children.

Once Paul learned the man was a coach who organized a youth basketball league and had lavished that same friend with football pads, cleats, and other costly gifts, he also detected an opportunity. Paul poured beer over his head and clothes, scratched gashes into his face, and warily stumbled into a nearby Catholic school gym during a game to attract the coach's attention.

The scheme worked. "I made myself look bad so he'd feel bad for me," Paul said. "He fell in love with me right there."

Paul joined the league and convinced Annie that his new coach was a positive influence. Months later, he moved into the man's apartment, and the *hustle* commenced.

Annie initially fell for the ruse, as did everyone. "I knew the guy, and I'd see him with Paul," said Paul's friend Brandon Cercone. "I didn't know he was a molester at the time."

Harry figured Paul was merely seeking something better. "I didn't really even think about it," he said. "The guy seemed okay at first, and all of our lives were rough."

And on the surface, things did improve. The coach bought Paul expensive sneakers and clothing. He paid to put braces on Paul's teeth and drove him around town. He treated Paul like an adult and allowed him to come and go as he pleased.

On the other hand, Paul was acutely mindful of the dangers in his new living arrangement. It started with the coach's amorous flirting and progressed with invitations to sit on his lap during basketball games, which Paul repeatedly spurned. It accelerated with his playful attempts to wrestle Paul on the living room carpet. One night, Paul walked downstairs and caught him rolling around with another kid in the dark. "No one ever said, 'Yo, he's touching me!'" Paul said. "People were scared and embarrassed."

Paul often heard the coach breathing outside his bathroom door and knew he was being watched while undressing, showering, and drying himself off. "He would look through the keyhole and see me naked," Paul explained. "But whenever I got done, I'd be able to get money from him and do whatever I wanted."

***

ROAD FROM PERDITION

Harry was introduced to boxing the afternoon Greg "Head" Linver brought him to Jack's, a boxing gym in Pittsburgh's rough-and-tumble Hill District neighborhood. Linver was once a three-time Golden Gloves Boxing Champion in three weight divisions.

He was also a family friend who suspected the oldest Spadafora boy would soak in the sights and sounds and take an immediate interest, much as he did during his formative years.

Linver's hunch proved correct. Harry was a natural competitor with an aggressive streak, and the gym became his playground. After picking up some amateur wins, Harry brought Paul along to watch one of his sparring sessions with noble intentions.

Harry knew Paul was an exceptional athlete and fearless when confronted physically. Paul needed to be tough because he did not fit in. "Paul had his hair dyed (bleach) blonde long before (the rapper) Eminem was even thought about, and he wore his hair in a Kid-n-Play (flat-top) box style because he went to a black barber who was well-known throughout Pittsburgh," described friend Justin Albrecht. "Paul was always beating kids up, but it wasn't always his fault. It was because they would tease him, saying he wanted to be black, not knowing those were the people we grew up around."

Albrecht said the beat-downs became so ruthless that Paul's teachers often sprayed him with hot water bottles to get him to stop. "When I used to get into fights on the streets, the first thing I'd say if I couldn't beat someone was, 'I'm going to get my cousin Paul to beat you up!'" Albrecht added.

Harry believed boxing could provide an outlet for Paul's aggression and add greater depth to his identity. In addition to Silvio's success as a Golden Gloves champ, their maternal grandfather, Eugene "Pap" Polecritti, competed as a Golden Gloves middleweight and worked as a sparring partner for Rocky Marciano. A distant cousin, Joey Maxim, was a former light-heavyweight champion who once scored a technical knockout over Sugar Ray Robinson.

But more essentially, Harry inferred the sport could provide structure and discipline – two fundamentals lacking from Paul's upbringing – and Golden Gloves titles could also lead to positive publicity, just as it had done for Linver, his Pap, and his father.

Paul was fascinated from the onset and continued to tag along with Harry. He was a natural righty but copied his brother's left-handed southpaw stance. Although his mechanics were sloppy, he was determined to learn. He could also eat a punch and keep going.

Sensing his potential, Paul took the Supplemental Security Income (SSI) check he had received monthly since his father's death and bought every boxing accessory he could find. "I was like, 'Fuck this! I'm gonna be a fighter!'" he exclaimed. "I spent every penny!"

Paul got additional rounds against different sparring partners at the old Hogan's Gym (formerly on Eighth Avenue in downtown Pittsburgh) and caught the attention of the gym's owner, Charles "P.K." Pecora. After observing Paul throw some punches, Pecora called Al McCauley, a friend and aspiring manager, with a bold declaration.

"You have to see this Spadafora kid!" Pecora said. "We have a future world champion right here!"

"Who, you mean Harry?" McCauley replied.

"No, his little brother, Paul!"

"How many fights does he have?"

"None."

McCauley chuckled but knew Pecora was not given to hyperbole.

Paul validated Pecora's intuition the following week. He timidly stepped between the ropes for his first amateur bout, all 112 pounds of skin and bone. Twenty minutes later, he strolled back to the locker room with the bounce of a world contender after taking a three-round decision.

His marriage to boxing became official that evening.

And then, the next day, it was nearly annulled when a trainer badgered Paul to drop his southpaw stance for a right-handed approach. The man was insistent, and Paul was annoyed. Paul was a beginner and respected the advice of any elder statesman, but his unconventional style fit him more snuggly than the Everlast gloves that protected his fists. It frustrated opponents into making mistakes. He had visions that it would help him achieve great things.

Paul mustered the courage to confront Pecora and complain, and, to his surprise, Pecora threw the antagonistic instructor out of his gym.

The interaction made Paul grin. It was so brief, so impactful, and as he would eventually come to learn, *so P.K.*

More saliently, it became the genesis of a relationship with the most meaningful influence in his lifetime.

***

Annie's suspicions of impropriety were piqued the morning she visited Paul at the coach's apartment and noticed wads of cotton stuffed in the keyholes of his bedroom and bathroom doors. When she found out her son had been drinking copious amounts of alcohol to reduce his discomfort, she connected the dots and pleaded with him to return home. Paul assured her he was in control and that his coach had never touched him. "If (the coach) started to get a little weird, I'd always put an immediate stop to it," he said.

Writing became Paul's escape. He immersed himself in an ongoing journal project that helped him make sense of the chaos. His "Books to God" became his release, his connection to a higher deity, and the words that spilled onto his stacks of paper regulated his sanity.

But whenever Paul needed physical distance, he would disappear entirely. Albrecht convinced his mom to let him stay at their home – sometimes for weeks. "I really didn't know what type of guy (the coach) was until we'd sleep over at his house, and Paul would tell him, 'Don't try no gay shit,'" Albrecht said.

Once Paul turned 13 and started dating his first girlfriend, he finally returned to his mom. Years later, the coach was arrested on two counts of statutory rape with a minor and was publicly outed as a sexual predator. "That guy was an extremely bad person – the worst," Paul said. "How bad can you be? This is what happens when you do the wrong thing as a little kid. I was taking advantage of a child molester, and I didn't have regrets about it then. I know I did the wrong thing by not doing anything, and some lives were destroyed because of it. It made me feel bad."

Paul was ready to feel good again and looked forward to re-establishing a sense of normalcy with his family, which would again prove impractical. Annie had moved to McKees Rocks, a ramshackle borough along the Ohio River. She tended bar at Mancini's Lounge, but tips were supplemented with cocaine sales that helped pay for groceries, electricity, and a new, chocolate-brown Cadillac. She had accumulated DUIs while Paul lived with the coach and did not tolerate banter about her new set of wheels, especially around the wrong company.

Harry learned Annie meant business the day she refused him the keys while her parole officer was en route. Rankled by her rejection, Harry said, "Hey Ma, you forgot to mention you're driving a new car!" when the man arrived.

Annie grabbed a knife from the kitchen, calmly walked into Harry's bedroom, and stabbed his hand to the top of a wooden dresser.

The parole officer slipped out the door amidst Harry's screams. After removing the blade from her son's bloody palm, Annie took him to the nearest emergency room, and he received several stitches.

The altercation exemplified a precarious period at the Spadafora residence. Annie continued dating a succession of men who treated her poorly, and her problems were exacerbated by her heavy drinking and the beginnings of a cocaine habit. The mayhem eventually drove Harry to move in with his (paternal) grandmother, Virginia Spadafore.

The absence of Charlie, who had been staying with Anthony's family, made Paul feel even lonelier. After escaping the clutches of a sex offender, he returned to a house that quickly became vacant.

Paul packed a bag and left Annie again. Learning from past mistakes, he found his own place – a one-bedroom apartment in a hardened sector of McKees Rocks called The Bottoms – and used his SSI aid to finance rent, food, and utilities.

A new entrepreneurial activity covered the rest.

Paul was 14 years old when he started cooking and distributing crack cocaine with classmates from Sto-Rox Middle School. He hid his inventory in baggies behind the light switches on his walls. It was a treacherous line of work that necessitated a pistol for protection, but it was also lucrative. Paul pocketed more than $600 one night with minimal effort. "We were all doing it to survive, to buy things like new shoes," Cercone said. "There were about four to six of us sleeping (at Paul's). It was the party house."

But the new lifestyle never turned out to be what Paul expected. He went into it believing it would be fun, yet hated interacting with junkies. He would see them deteriorate before his eyes and knew he played a role in their misery. He felt tremendous guilt and stopped dealing after several weeks. "I'd tell these people, 'You need help. I'm giving you this drug, and you're coming back to me looking like this, and you want more, so I keep giving it to you,'" Paul said. "I was living my own life, but I was doing the wrong thing."

Harry disapproved but empathized. "When you don't have anything, it's a different world compared to kids who have a chance," he said. "Kids who don't know any better can't teach themselves how to always do the right thing. When you're young, and you have nothing, and the only way you can get things is through friends, who become your family, that's where you go."

But Paul *always* had another place, a sanctuary from his suffering, an oasis of stability, a beacon of light that could guide him through the anguish and despair.

***

ROAD FROM PERDITION

"P.K." was short for "Pittsburgh Kid," a nickname originally held by East Liberty native Billy Conn and later adopted by Pecora when he competed as an amateur. Conn (63-11-1, 15 knockouts) had always been Pecora's favorite fighter during an era in western Pennsylvania when the volume of elite boxing talent almost matched its steel export.

Braddock's Frank Klaus and New Castle's George Chip dominated the middleweight ranks and captured world titles before the start of World War I. They preceded Garfield's Harry Greb, also known as "The Pittsburgh Windmill," due to his abnormal ability to fire a frenetic flurry of haymakers from multiple angles. Greb held the American Light Heavyweight Championship (1922 to 1923) and the World Middleweight Championship (1923 to 1926) and is forever embedded in the pantheon of the sport's pound-for-pound punching megastars.

After the North Side's Teddy Yarosz won the middleweight crown in 1934, five western Pennsylvania fighters held world titles in five of the eight traditional weight classes at different times between 1939 and 1941. The famed group, led by Conn (at lightweight), included Washington's Sammy Angott (lightweight), Lawrenceville's Fritzie Zivic (welterweight), Farrell's Billy Soose (middleweight), and Pittsburgh's Jackie Wilson (featherweight). Add local luminaries like Braddock's Buck McTiernan and Jimmy Belmont (middle and welterweights), East Liberty's Carmen Notch (a welterweight and Zivic's main sparring partner), and Charley Burley – a black middleweight from the Hill District whom some historians consider the greatest boxer never to get a title shot – and the list of names becomes extraordinary.

Conn, in particular, always held a special place in Pecora's heart. Quick hands, fleet feet, and textbook-accurate technique helped him defeat nine world champions in three weight divisions by age 23.

His audacity, nonetheless, made him an exhilarating fighter, as revealed in his fabled 1941 match with Joe Louis. Despite moving up a weight class and surrendering more than 25 pounds, Conn stymied Louis as the bout proceeded, slithering inside to unload a barrage of combos before switching angles and floating away like an apparition to elude his opponent's murderous power. Conn drilled Louis with punishing blows in rounds 11 and 12 and led on the scorecards. He was in the driver's seat to secure an upset for the ages, and the crowd at New York's Polo Grounds loved every second.

But that, as legend has it, was all before adrenaline and pride got the better of him. Conn went to his corner and told manager Johnny Ray that he would knock Louis out in the thirteenth, and Ray's pleas to stick with the blueprint fell on deaf ears. Conn was determined to swing for the fences and would not be convinced otherwise.

Moments later, he stood up, went toe-to-toe with one of the most intimidating punchers in boxing history, and paid the price. Louis smacked Conn with a right cross to the jaw. He followed with a mix of body shots before dropping Conn with a beastly right in the waning seconds. Conn could not beat the count, and the ref called the bout, capping off a tension-filled contest that ranks sixth-best on *The Ring* magazine's all-time list of greatest fights.

Conn met with reporters and sardonically summed up his stubbornness by remarking, "What's the use of being Irish if you can't be dumb?" Although his *damn the torpedoes, full speed ahead* objective may have been ill-conceived, it was never in Conn's nature to avoid challenges. His dedication toward beating Louis at his own game was seen as inspiring to many. He dared to be great and, as a result, is remembered as one of the greatest.

Pecora knew little about the scrawny Spadafora kid who demanded to fight as a lefty but wondered if he might be witnessing something uniquely similar. Apart from his uncanny resemblance to the Steel City icon who nearly toppled "the Brown Bomber," other similarities were beginning to emerge.

Harry was a brawler who could pummel opponents into submission. He won frequently with a booming left and moved on to capture the first of his three Western Pennsylvania Golden Gloves Titles (in the 147- and 156-pound weight classes) over six years. Though Paul also possessed power, he was more determined to replicate Harry's success with reflexive counterpunching, which flourished under Pecora. Harry had an anvil chin and could scrap with the best of them, but Paul's most noteworthy assets were his intelligence, confidence, and willingness to learn.

Some of Paul's earliest lessons came from the fists of Eric Podolak, a prolific amateur who turned pro in the super lightweight division. They sparred thousands of rounds, and Podolak often sent him limping away. It never bothered Pecora. He knew the lumps Paul took would only make him wiser. "(Podolak) was the one who taught me how to fight," Paul said. "He beat me really hard."

Albrecht had never seen Paul back away from any challenge in the hallways of their middle school, and the gym was no different. "(Paul) would go all the way to Monroeville to spar this older, bigger guy named Dan Connelly who used to fight Harry," Albrecht said. "This dude was an adult (and a Golden Gloves champion), and Paul would really give him a run for his money."

And it was all due to his assiduous attention to detail. "(Harry) taught me what I shouldn't do from his mistakes, like how you don't drop your right hand when you throw your left hand because that's how you get caught," Paul said. "I always looked up to him."

But from his earliest experiences at Hogan's, it was Pecora he wanted to impress most. On the streets, Paul was a menace. In the ring, he was an apt pupil, sniper-focused on devouring every morsel of Pecora's curriculum. Progress meant little unless the old professor was watching. He hungered for his approval. It was something he never received from his father. "P.K. told me he waited 50 years for a kid like me to walk into his gym," Paul said. "When I went there, I knew P.K. was going to be there, and I was going to be fighting. In order to keep P.K. there, I had to do what I had to do."

And that was to keep improving at an exponential pace. By age 15, Paul had followed in Harry's footsteps by winning his first Western Pennsylvania Golden Gloves title. That summer, he also won three consecutive decisions to place first in the 125-pound single-elimination division of the Ohio State Fair National Boxing Tournament, widely regarded as one of the top amateur testing grounds in the nation.

With Pecora by his side, Paul felt unbeatable. He even began entertaining a lofty goal that would have once seemed outrageous to a young hooligan scraping to get by in the dingy back alleys of Pittsburgh's roughest neighborhoods.

One day, he would become a world champion.

Chapter 4: P.K.'s Prodigy

Paul transferred to Shaler Area High School in 1991 at the beginning of his freshman year. He lived with his Uncle Paul, who worked as a Spanish teacher in the building. Shaler had a solid academic reputation and was located in a more affluent region of Pittsburgh. Paul's family believed a new environment could give him a fresh start.

As a bonus, enrollment would also allow him to pursue one of his other passions.

Paul made an immediate impression during pre-season workouts for the Shaler basketball team that fall. His dribbling was smooth; his outside jumper was silky. He was young and undersized but talented enough to earn a spot on the varsity roster.

His coaches, opposingly, were peeved with his laissez-faire attitude. Paul would *borrow* his uncle's car to attend practice and almost always arrived late. On occasion, he would skip practice entirely. One evening, he barely caught the bus as it pulled out of the school parking lot to transport the team to an early-season opponent and then, before taking a seat, realized his uniform was hanging in his gym locker. Paul was a standout middle-schooler who had once dropped 45 points in a game. He was also unreliable. After being told he would not play, a fiery assistant snarled, "This is not junior high anymore! This is the big leagues!"

Paul's cavalier disposition toward practice spilled into his classes – whenever he attended them. He spent part of each morning learning about female anatomy in the building's empty auditorium with the help of a scantily dressed co-ed. Interest in valid academic pursuits dwindled, and he barely maintained passing grades.

The Shaler experiment fizzled completely when Paul quit basketball after being barred from traveling to Florida with the team for a Christmas tournament. He finished the year at Langley High School, which is footnoted as another temporary stop in an educational journey that had been crumbling for years.

Paul's home life was no better. He moved back in with Annie again, but she was drinking heavily. Annie fell behind on her rent and was soon evicted from her apartment. Paul stayed with friends while she searched for new accommodations. He once slept under a relative's porch for several weeks with the family dog, a Doberman named "Rocco."

"I did not want his family to know I was there because I did not want to burden them," he said.

Paul registered at Sto-Rox High School as a sophomore and found it challenging to take his new course load seriously – with one exception.

Sue Pecori taught English. She believed in rules but also made learning fresh and exciting. She enthused Paul to open a book and pay attention. Because of her prodding, he applied himself and earned his first "B."

"It was obvious that Paul liked my class, and he did not have a problem coming to it," Pecori said. "When he was there, he was never a problem. He was never anything but polite."

Pecori would watch Paul jog the undulating hills of McKees Rocks each morning before pulling into the school parking lot to begin her workday. "The home life was not good, and it was obvious school was not his thing," she explained. "(Paul's) only goals were in relation to sports. I tried to put my finger on why someone like him would be so willing to come into my room and be like he was, and it's probably because I was very structured and a strong disciplinarian. Boxing required so much discipline, and I think the structure and discipline of my class were good for him. He didn't object to it."

Paul only objected to the rest of a rigorous academic schedule that kept him from the boxing gym, and Pecori could not teach him every subject. He joined the Sto-Rox basketball team, but even that could not distract him from his true obsession. "When Paul was at school, he could only think about being a boxing champion," Cercone said. "It blocked everything else out. So he was there (physically), but he really wasn't there (mentally). He knew he was going to be a champion one day, but he just had to wait it out. It was already decided in his head."

The strife Paul encountered scholastically and domestically had little bearing on his evolution as a fighter. Pecora drove Paul to Western Penitentiary and watched him pad his record with victories over inmates. In a short time, he would even win over the respect of North American Boxing Association (NABF) featherweight champion Harold Rhodes. Paul and Harry sparred Rhodes at Jack's in the afternoons before Hogan's opened its doors in the evenings. "They both would take turns beating on (Rhodes)," said Rhodes's trainer, Kevin "Leroy" Scotty. "Paul especially used to give him fits."

Paul helped Lamar Williams (5-1-1 record at welterweight) prepare for his professional bout against Oscar de la Hoya. Williams remembers being amazed. "Here Paul was only 16 years old, and I'm thinking, *I'm gonna beat the hell outta this poor little white boy*,"

Williams said. "But man, did he give me the business! (Paul) was one of the hardest people to hit in the world."

As it became evermore apparent Paul would never attend college or work a nine-to-five job behind a desk, Pecora cleared the air. "I really liked basketball, but as soon as P.K. told me, 'You're not going to ever make the NBA,' it was over!" Paul said. "As soon as he put that in my head, (P.K.) changed my perspective completely."

Paul dropped out of school that same week and swore his life to the ring. He commemorated the occasion with his first tattoo – the word "SOUTH" etched over a paw print on his upper stomach. The design was an oath to commit himself to the unorthodox stance he fought so fervently to preserve in one of his first conversations with Pecora, a sage mentor who had become his biggest supporter.

***

Paul loved drinking, and beer was his biggest vice. Stories circulated about Paul polishing off entire cases of Budweiser in one sitting. Pecora knew alcoholism ran rampant in the Spadafora bloodline and scolded Paul whenever he caught him indulging.

Pecora also realized it was easier for Paul to kick the bottle when he was kept busy throwing his hands. During training camps, Paul even turned down invitations to smoke marijuana at parties, knowing it would impair his conditioning.

Keeping Paul engaged through boxing cured everything. After winning another regional Golden Gloves title, Paul traveled to York, Pennsylvania, and defeated John Scalzi to win the 1993 Pennsylvania Golden Gloves

P.K.'S PRODIGY

Championship at 132 pounds, along with "Outstanding Boxer of the Tournament" accolades.

He continued to chase Harry, who had received national acclaim at 156 pounds after earning a bronze medal in the USA Boxing Federation Championship. A broken nose in his 7-4 quarterfinal win over Portland's Timothy Mudgett forced Harry to forfeit his semifinal bout against Miami's Wayne Blair, officially killing his chances to contend for a national title. But Harry skipped competing in the Pennsylvania Golden Gloves Tournament championship to represent Team USA in its exhibition against Team Canada and split two bouts against Bernard Pinnoseault.

On the whole, things were looking up for the Spadafora tandem.

And they were about to get even better for Paul.

Four labral-tear shoulder injuries derailed Tom Yankello's amateur boxing career, so he pursued the next best option and became a trainer. He began working with fighters at Beaver County Boxing Club, but after driving his top amateurs to Hogan's in 1993, he became acquainted with Paul and Harry. "I was impressed with how dedicated they were with coming to the gym," Yankello said. "They were the talk of the city in the amateur scene."

Yankello focused on the lightweights and pitted Paul against Scott McCracken – his top fighter. McCracken showed loads of promise and packed dynamite in his balled-up fists. The two sparred regularly and became fast friends. "Scotty could fight – whoa!" Paul said. "Mean right hand. He hurt me maybe only five times, but when he did, it was really bad."

Those competitive scuffles also helped Paul bond with Yankello. Though only three years his senior, Yankello was an old soul with the maturity of a trainer who had been in the fight game for decades. He was a creative tactician, well-adjusted at tailoring his instruction to each boxer's strengths and personality.

Besides McCracken, Yankello tutored Verquan Kimbrough, a star-in-the-making at 112 pounds. McCracken and Kimbrough aspired to become world champions and entrusted Yankello to guide them to the summit.

Pecora respected Yankello's insight and encouraged Paul to listen and learn. To his credit, Paul was always a receptive student – that is what made him good. But as Yankello discovered, his clairvoyance made him exceptional. "Paul's physical speed was fantastic, but his mental speed was even more so," Yankello said. "His ability to process information... you could just see that early on. He was always setting you up. He always knew what his next move would be."

Paul returned to Philadelphia in 1994 and scored a unanimous decision over Steve D'Martino to win his second consecutive Pennsylvania Golden Gloves Title at 132 pounds. He carried that momentum into the U.S. National Golden Gloves Championships in Milwaukee later that year, intending to lock in a national ranking, just as Harry had done a year prior.

Although his attempt fell flat when he dropped an opening-round decision to Salvador Jasso, the eventual winner of the lightweight bracket, the experience was not a total loss.

Floyd Mayweather Jr. joined Paul in the elevator of a hotel housing the competitors. Mayweather had previously taken the Golden Gloves National Title at 106 pounds and was searching for a second championship at 112.

As Paul pressed the button to his floor, he claimed Mayweather asked him whom he was fighting.

Paul replied, "Salvador Jasso," and returned the question. He alleged Mayweather blurted, "I'm not fighting anyone. I'm knocking everyone out! I knocked everyone out at 106, and I'm going to knock everyone out at 112!"

Mayweather partially backed his bravado by later scoring a decision over Linton Nichols to win the 112-pound championship. And the following year, he mowed through the 126-pound bracket to win his third consecutive national amateur title.

He was brazen, boisterous, and bombastic. But he was also intelligent, mind-blowingly quick, and suitably called "Pretty Boy" because he *never* seemed to get hit.

All the same, Paul never considered him to be in a different league, and he began to salivate over the prospect of meeting Mayweather in the ring.

This desire, made possible by an unexpected encounter, would drive Paul to make it a reality.

***

Regardless of the experience level of the man standing across from him, Paul felt omnipotent. "Paul's life was in complete disarray outside of boxing, but the reason he trained the way he trained is because he fell in love with boxing," Yankello said. "(The ring) was where everything was okay. Paul didn't have to think about all of his outside problems. It was peaceful. His passion for the sport was the only thing that was normal in his life."

But the gym, unfortunately, could not stay open 24 hours, and Paul's promotional team could not organize weekly bouts. The lapses drove Paul to drink from dusk till dawn, wake up at noon, and repeat the cycle the following evening.

On December 23, 1994, it culminated in a humbling experience that made Paul contemplate the consequences of his actions.

Paul was a passenger in a car driven by a friend. Both had been drinking and were well above the legal limit. A police officer tailed them and turned on his red-and-blue lights.

When the friend asked what they should do, Paul yelled, "Motherfucker! The cops are behind you! You better get us out of here! I'm not trying to get pulled over!"

A high-speed chase ensued down a narrow neighborhood street before the driver lost control and crashed into a telephone pole.

Things turned catastrophic when a cop approached the passenger's side door and instructed Paul and his friend to exit the vehicle before unintentionally discharging his gun.

"I didn't even get a chance to open the door," Paul said. "It was POP-POP-POP – just like that – and (my friend) screamed, 'You've been shot!'"

Paul's left Timberland boot filled with blood and soaked into the floormat. He was loaded into an ambulance minutes after his enraged buddy was wrestled into a squad car and taken to the station.

As the alcohol wore off, Paul's lower calf began to feel like it had been crammed through a woodchipper. His post-surgery prognosis was even more painful. The bullet had sliced into his Achilles tendon, and doctors told him he would be lucky to walk again without a cane, let alone box.

Pecora knew better. Though disappointed Paul had ruined any likelihood of earning a spot on the 1996 U.S. Olympic Boxing Team, his knee was not damaged. And after six months in a cast, Paul defied doctors' orders and resurrected his training with his running. He pushed through the pulsating soreness and logged hundreds of miles between Carnegie and Carlynton as he regained his stamina.

When Paul returned to the gym, the real work began. The injury diminished Paul's leverage to pivot when throwing a punch from his left leg, consequently lessening the force behind his left fist. "There's no doubt (Paul) hit harder before he got shot," Yankello said. "And he was more aggressive when he had that power."

The strength behind Paul's body shots was still potent, and his hand speed and mental acuity remained better than ever. With Yankello's assistance, Pecora set out to cultivate these traits and shape Paul into an old-school boxer in the template of Conn. He prodded Paul to combine agility with continual head movement, encouraging him to slip outside to score points with his rangy jab. But should anyone venture too close, Pecora also primed Paul to be in a perfect position to make opponents pay with hooks and uppercuts to the ribs. "Paul knew what he wanted to do, and he knew what your reaction was going to be to it, so then he already knew the counter," Yankello said. "Paul knew if he would throw this punch, this is the position his opponent would be in, and then he would capitalize and be able to create an opening."

This prescient ring acumen set him apart. "(Pecora) gave me the eye," Paul said. "He taught me how to be safe, careful, and cautious. People might headbutt me a little, but they could never hit me."

Amidst his comeback, Paul filed a lawsuit and won a summary judgment against the police department for the shooting incident. He would also get his second tattoo – a thorn necklace connected by boxing gloves – encircling his shoulders and upper chest. He would gaze at it in the mirror each morning and remind himself to make better choices.

Paul ached to fight as he watched Harry win his first Pennsylvania Golden Gloves title that summer with a unanimous decision over Chris Walsh at 156 pounds.

With his mind, body, and spirit in a better place, Paul made his highly anticipated return to the Ohio State Fair in August of 1995. He erased any doubt by again taking first place, this time with a convincing unanimous decision over Tony Wall in the 132-pound final.

Former World Boxing Federation (WBF) Super Middleweight Champion "Iceman" John Scully was working Wall's corner. "Tony was a really good fighter," Scully recalled, "but Spadafora was just on another level."

The victory fortified Paul's confidence to become the world's best lightweight. It steadied his determination to maintain his sobriety and follow the rules.

The future, he believed, looked brighter than ever.

After the referee raised his arm, Paul glanced at Pecora, flashed a megawatt grin, and shouted, "Fuck it, P.K.! We're turning pro!"

Chapter 5: Ballrooms and Boxing Gloves

There was no fanfare the day Paul signed a professional contract with Pecora. Any acknowledgment was kept to a minimum. But Paul remembered his grueling hours at the gym throughout the following weeks. He took long runs each morning before he worked the heavy bag and sparred away entire afternoons against Yankello's skilled stable of boxers.

And then there was his homework. Pecora sent Paul away each night with boxes of VHS tapes containing bundles of fight footage. Paul would study "classic" bouts featuring Ricardo Lopez, Salvadore Sánchez, and Roberto Duran into the wee hours of the morning, along with grainy clips of Billy Conn, Fritzie Zivic, and Charley Burley. "Those guys way back in the day, in order to fight for world titles, had to be really up there," Paul said. "Nowadays, it's totally different. Who you know helps a ton more."

Paul knew Pecora, and that was the only person who mattered. Pecora was to Paul what Cus D'Amato was to Mike Tyson. Harry brought Paul to the ring, but Pecora helped him realize his potential to be phenomenal.

And the relationship extended beyond boxing.

Whenever Paul was not crashing with friends, he lodged with Pecora and his wife, Rachael, and enjoyed dinner with their family. Pecora bought Paul new clothes and shoes and helped cover Annie's rent and utility payments. He ensured Paul was well-supported to concentrate on becoming a better fighter and, in the long run, a better man.

Paul naturally wanted to make Pecora proud, and his self-confidence skyrocketed into new stratospheres. This unveiled itself on October 18, 1995, the evening he made his professional debut. Paul shook his head in frustration as he sat in the Pittsburgh Sheraton at Station Square dressing room. He was slated to meet Steve Maddux (2-11) on the undercard of the main event that pitted Arthur "Babyface" Allen against Reggie Strickland. Allen (17-1-1, five knockouts) was a world super welterweight contender managed by McCauley, but Paul believed *he* should have been the featured attraction. "These motherfuckers can't fight like me!" he crowed to Cercone. "There is no better fighter here! People came to see me! Watch, you'll all see!"

Paul slipped Maddux's best punches and adroitly countered with jabs and body shots to take an easy four-round unanimous decision and a check for $200. "Fifty dollars for each round," Paul said matter-of-factly. "P.K. always told me to never spend my fight money, and I was basically homeless. But I didn't have to worry that I was going to go back and sell crack. I knew then that I was a fighter."

A month later, Paul scored a resounding second-round technical knockout over Nathanial Hardy (2-10) on the Hector Camacho – Danny Chavez undercard in The Harv at Mountaineer Casino Racetrack & Resort in Chester, West Virginia.

The night was exceptionally momentous for Harry, who recorded a second-round technical knockout in his pro debut over Tom McCain. As Paul watched his older brother fight, he appreciated the occasion's magnitude. Six years earlier, they were a couple of street urchins exploring a new hobby. And here they were, slugging it out, side-by-side, attempting to carve out careers as professional boxers.

Somehow, against all odds, they emerged from the cigarette ashes of their adolescence and were making a name for themselves, one punch at a time.

Paul won unanimously over Anthony Hardy (3-15-1) in Erie, Pennsylvania. He closed the year at the Holiday Inn Metroplex in Liberty, Ohio, with a first-round knockout over Lacebian Crocket (0-5).

At 4-0 with two knockouts, he knew he needed to build up his record with at least 10 more wins before anyone would take him seriously. Paul became obsessed with his training and realized exposure on a national stage would be his only shot at making headway.

A childhood friend who worked as Paul's first manager helped get him on the undercard of the February 20, 1996, Roberto Duran vs. Ray Domenge headliner on *USA Network's Tuesday Night Fights*. His opponent – Michael Lopez – posed no threat at 1-6.

Paul only hoped the bout would air, confident his ability would take care of the rest. He entered Miami's Mahi Temple Shrine Auditorium wearing yellow trunks with red trim and an icy countenance that belied his inexperience. And by the second round, he looked every part of a savvy veteran who belonged in front of cameras when he bashed Lopez with a left that sent him tottering against the ropes.

But it was not until midway through the third that Paul truly imposed his will, catching Lopez with another left before landing a bone-rattling right that busted open his nose and knocked him onto his rear end. When Lopez returned to his feet, Paul shelled him again with several more punches, forcing Lopez's corner to stop the fight before the fourth. "The (Lopez) kid was hitting Paul with some shots he never should have hit him with, but all in all, Paul did really well," Yankello said.

Paul only made $150 and quipped he needed it to "pay his way to get home."

Even so, he got his wish.

McCauley's "Babyface" Allen lost in the co-main event to Santiago Samaniego by second-round technical knockout, which opened a spot to televise Paul's performance.

And as McCauley watched Paul box, he thought about Pecora's phone call from several years earlier.

You have to check out this Spadafora kid! We have a future world champion right here!

***

Yankello rehabbed his shoulders and joined McCracken in Paul's sparring rotation as part of a last-ditch attempt to revamp his amateur career. He carried a 16-8 record at 147 pounds and entertained aspirations of turning pro. Nevertheless, Yankello's comeback hit the wall when he retore his labrum a fifth time after only a few months of work, and he was forced to stop competing for good.

Harry, meanwhile, decided to quit for preventative reasons. Since his early days at Jack's, he embraced the visceral violence boxing offered and enjoyed searching for each knockout. It was a gallant tactic that brought him remarkable success.

But it was also dangerous. Harry worried about becoming "punch-drunk." And when his girlfriend gave birth to his son only months after he made his pro debut, he opted to provide for his new family through a more sensible job in construction.

BALLROOMS AND BOXING GLOVES

Although the brother act was ending in the gym, Paul understood Harry's reasoning and wanted to start a family of his own. He presumed he was well on his way only weeks after the Lopez win when his girlfriend of seven years gave birth to a baby girl. The idea of fatherhood delighted him. Paul made plans to get married and believed his life was progressing accordingly.

The excitement, however, blinded him to the startling details of the delivery.

Paul's girlfriend was Caucasian, but the baby had dark pigmentation. When Paul's friends pointed out the resemblance between the infant and Paul's first manager – a black man – it coerced him to confront her and demand a paternity test.

The results substantiated Paul's suspicions and wrecked his world. The shock of it caught him days later after a morning jog. He slumped on his mom's porch and cried. "Whenever you get hurt like that, as soon as you shut the door, you're gone," Paul said. "I was ready to go crazy, catch a homicide, do all that bullshit. I'm a person who can certainly do the wrong thing to someone when I'm mad. I hadn't done anything wrong, and I was the one who got hurt."

Paul's grandfather found him and offered a unique perspective on the longevity of the failed relationship. As Pap put it, Paul never really knew his girlfriend when he first met her or even at the very end. When she and the child left his house, Pap said Paul should consider them gone forever.

He then went on to demonstrate his commitment to Paul's well-being.

"(Pap) goes inside, pulled out a gun, and tells me, 'If anyone comes onto this porch to hurt you, I'm blowing their fucking head off!'"

Paul befriended the same woman years later, but the conversation with his Pap hardened him. "I knew I would never allow myself to be hurt by a female again."

***

Cercone drove Paul to Ocean City, Maryland, to pull him out of his funk. Pecora grew weary of the drama. He was sympathetic to Paul's plight, but his ultimatum was stern. "If you ain't home by Monday," he said, "your rent isn't gonna be paid for!"

Paul was miserable but wisely came to his senses. "I had to book," he said. "P.K. was someone you don't fuck with, a real person who loved me like a son, who took care of me like a son. My mom was strung out, my brother was living at my grandma's (house), and my panic level was at an all-time high. Without P.K., I was scared because I knew he was the only guy I ever trusted and the only guy who would get me the big fights."

Once home, Paul took a quantum leap forward by appointing McCauley as his new manager. In addition to Allen, McCauley had been shepherding the career of Tim Williamson (an amateur light heavyweight who was months away from capturing a 1996 National Golden Gloves Championship). McCauley was driven to get the most out of his fighters and believed he was sitting on a winning lottery ticket with Pecora's protégé.

Just as beneficial as having a stalwart manager was having a reputable promoter. Paul found one in Erie native Mike Acri, who was touted as one of boxing's hottest up-and-coming matchmakers.

BALLROOMS AND BOXING GLOVES

With his new brain trust assembled, Paul fought Julio Ibarra (9-17, four knockouts) in March. After plodding through the first round, Paul gradually reestablished his dominance and won by technical knockout in the third. "(Paul) screwed up a little in this fight in the beginning," McCauley explained, "but after that, P.K. had him stay on point."

Paul dropped to super featherweight (130 pounds) that May and defeated Erik Joshua (0-2-3) by unanimous decision. In June, he cut down further to featherweight (125) and finished Calvin Faggins (3-2-1) by technical knockout. Paul bounced back to super featherweight two weeks later and picked up a unanimous decision against Antonio Gonzalez (3-14-2) on the Roberto Duran – Hector Camacho undercard in Atlantic City.

From there, the wins piled up. Paul tallied technical knockouts over Jeff Whaley (18-34-1, one knockout) on the September Roberto Duran – Mike Culbert undercard and against Mark Andreske (4-5-1, two knockouts) in an October lightweight bout. He stopped Greg McLean (0-1) on December 22 with a body shot midway through the second in their super featherweight matchup to finish 1996 at 12-0 with eight stoppages.

Although the victories came against palookas who ate punches for paltry payouts, Paul's televised dominance over Lopez put him on the map, and his unblemished record put his name on every promoter's lips. "You have to make the ring your home where you are so comfortable," he said. "I ain't ever seen anyone as comfortable as me in the ring. I'm as comfortable as you can get."

The Spadafora team became a four-headed monster. McCauley and Acri searched and scheduled. Pecora prepared.

Paul won.

They felt unstoppable.

***

Pecora suffered a stroke and was admitted to Allegheny General Hospital in late January 1997. The news ruffled Paul, but Pecora assured him he would return to the gym soon.

Early into his recovery, Pecora assigned Yankello to prepare Paul for his March super featherweight match against Joe Lafontant (3-6-1, one knockout), which would be part of the Sugar Ray Leonard – Hector Camacho undercard in Atlantic City.

Yankello was a realistic substitution because he was still training McCracken, a first-rate sparring partner who would only make Paul better. He also had opened his eponymous Tom Yankello's World Class Boxing Gym in Ambridge and had attracted a sizable following.

But more than anything, Pecora wanted Yankello to fill in because he respected his intellect.

Paul struggled dropping to 130 pounds. At 5-foot-9, he was a squid-like presence with whip-like limbs, making him almost impossible to reach. At the same time, he was also winded and weaker by the middle rounds.

Pecora delivered on his promise and returned to help Paul complete his training camp. A week later, Paul barely made the lighter weight class and only squeaked past Lafontant on points.

Paul sulked afterward as he watched Camacho win an electrifying fifth-round technical knockout over Leonard.

BALLROOMS AND BOXING GLOVES

He did not feel indestructible – at least not as he had been in previous fights. It left Pecora questioning whether his fighter's excessive eating, boozing, and extreme weight loss would have disastrous ramifications.

That May, Acri moved Paul up to the 140-pound super lightweight division to take on Julio Cesar Merino (3-10-2, one knockout). The weight allowance enabled Paul to pack greater force behind his punches, and it helped him score a first-round technical knockout. "Paul beat that kid's ass and looked great," Yankello said.

The win – his fourteenth in the record books – was earned in the main event of a small card in Ridgeway, a three-hour drive from downtown Pittsburgh. On paper, it was a trivial contest that Paul expected would lead to better things.

But in little time, the bout would become a memento mori, and its haunting significance would remind Paul to embrace each experience because the next day is never guaranteed.

***

Pecora had a second stroke and was hospitalized in late July. He dismissed its severity again and told Paul he would be fine following surgery.

Days later, Paul's universe imploded after returning home from a sparring session and learning Pecora's health had worsened. Vehicle-less, Paul ran – for more than four miles from his front door on The North Side to the sliding glass doors of the emergency room at UPMC Presbyterian in Oakland. He arrived drenched in sweat, panting, and choking back sobs. "(The news) hit me like a ton of bricks," Paul said. "I was just lost and didn't really know what to do because P.K. was like a dad. At the time, he was the only guy I was ever gonna listen to."

Pecora passed away on July 27, 1997. The wake was well-attended, a testament to his popularity. Paul woefully did his best to shake hands and exchange condolences. Pecora had meant the world to him for more than eight years. He longed to relive their final moments during his last fight. They seemed so transient, undervalued, and wasted.

That afternoon, Acri and McCauley brought Yankello to a coffee shop across the street from the funeral home and conducted an impromptu job interview. Paul expressed interest in retaining Yankello as his trainer. Yankello was ambitious and knowledgeable, but he was also 26. Acri preferred an older presence like Pat Burns, who was training Camacho in Florida and was open to adding a new fighter.

Then again, Acri also knew Yankello had been influential in helping Pecora refine Paul's technique.

McCauley had never met Yankello before the viewing but was aware Pecora endorsed him. He also realized Paul needed a robust support system that would show tough love.

"Paul wanted Tommy, and a fighter should get what a fighter wants," McCauley said. "I was the one who said let's give this guy a chance, and Mike respected my opinion. Tommy had worked hard, and I never had a problem with him. He was good with me, so I thought we should give him a shot."

McCauley had already forged a financial partnership with Pecora's friends – Al Monzo and Jim Rizzo – to help bankroll Paul's career. Monzo hosted fight cards in the banquet room of his Palace Inn hotel in nearby

BALLROOMS AND BOXING GLOVES

Monroeville. All three were interested in helping Paul finish what Pecora had started.

Yankello knew he also had to make a deeper investment to get the most out of a prospective champion. "P.K. and Paul had a lot of love for each other," Yankello said. "You could see a special bond that went far beyond a boxer and a boxing trainer. P.K. took over that father role that Paul never had. Paul connected with him. (Pecora) brought Paul around his family, took him under his wing, and really looked out for him. P.K. was a surrogate dad."

And that is why Paul grieved.

Hard.

As he looked down at the old man in the coffin for the last time, a piece of him went with Pecora.

***

If Pecora invented Paul's innovative fighting style, Yankello could be credited with polishing it to near perfection. The shooting injury had decreased the power behind Paul's left hand, and Yankello cringed when he reverted to squaring up. It stirred Yankello to elevate Paul's defense in the mold of Floyd Mayweather Jr. and one of Paul's boxing heroes, Pernell Whitaker.

"(Paul) was always a respectable puncher, but he was no longer going to be a dominant puncher, so he really didn't need to be in that phonebooth kind of fight," Yankello said. "Paul was a very tall lightweight. He had great inside skills, but I angled Paul off even more and got him to sit back and raise his right shoulder so he'd be able to utilize his height and reach and step around guys."

Paul looked lost without Pecora during his early rounds against Bernard Harris, a capable lightweight with an 11-2-1 record and six knockouts.

Yankello finally got him to relax and implement their refined strategy, and Paul earned a unanimous decision against the sturdiest fighter he had yet encountered. "(Paul) was on the inside but was still half the target, and I felt he was starting to angle himself better," Yankello said. "He was being half of a target instead of being squared off, and positioning is everything."

Paul looked so good that Yankello began counting the number of victories he would need to land a top-10 ranking. After cruising past Kino Rodriguez (9-12-2, one knockout) via unanimous decision on the Oscar De La Hoya – Hector Camacho undercard in Las Vegas, Paul dropped Hector Ramirez (12-26, six knockouts) with a left hand in the second round of their October bout at Monzo's Palace Inn in Monroeville to go 16-0. "Paul had a complex that he no longer hit hard enough after his injury," Yankello said. "He'd go into these fights as more of a pure boxer, but he sometimes had a hard time knocking people out, and he always wanted to do that. So when he scored that knockout, he was happy as shit."

Paul concluded 1997 with a December tilt against Roger Brown at the Avalon Hotel in Erie. Brown's record of 13-17 with five knockouts appeared unexceptional, but he posted strong showings against a lineup of champions that included Frankie Randall, Tracy Spann, James "Buddy" McGirt, Edwin Rosario, and Jose Luis Ramirez. He also had twice defeated former IBF lightweight titleholder Harry Arroyo.

Brown had a bulldog's body but fought like a Rottweiler, and he was unfazed by the hype surrounding Paul. He made this known in the early rounds as he unloaded a maelstrom of haymakers. "I remember Paul weaving under and rolling shots that went – *WHOOSH* –

right past him," Yankello said. "You're like, *Damn! If that shot catches him, it could hurt him!*"

Paul never flinched. "You had your concern, but Paul had radar," Yankello added. "He had an ability to anticipate a punch and see it coming, and he was always in the right position, too. Positioning beats speed, and Paul was so cerebrally fast."

And determined. Paul outboxed Brown for the remainder of the fight to win unanimously. "I was always a good ring general," Paul said. "I always knew where to be and what to do next. If I made a single mistake and my opponent cracked me once, it would never happen again."

Later that night, Yankello drove into a dense snowstorm on his trip home to Ambridge. The visibility along Pennsylvania's Interstate 79 became so poor that he could barely see 10 feet beyond the hood of his Chevy Malibu.

Nonetheless, as he gripped the steering wheel and cautiously slogged down the highway, he remembered his vision becoming crystal clear. "In my head, I'm thinking it's all going to be worth it because this kid can be a champion, and I just gotta keep working my ass off because (Paul) is going to put me on the map," Yankello said. "I always knew he could really be something special."

***

Paul kicked off 1998 at Monzo's that March with a unanimous decision victory over Troy Fletcher (13-5-2, two knockouts).

Two months later, he returned to the same ballroom to meet Amado Cabato, a seasoned journeyman with a 47-26-8 record and 23 knockouts. Paul landed a torrent of combos to stop Cabato by technical knockout in the seventh round and seamlessly cruised to his twentieth win.

McCauley praised Yankello for doing an admirable job as Pecora's successor, to which Yankello replied, "(Paul) is only going to get even better."

The number on the scale, disconcertingly, often loomed larger than the opponent. Paul nearly forfeited against Puerto Rico's Jose Aponte in their June 23, 1998 headliner for the vacant International Boxing Council (IBC) America's Lightweight Title at The Harv because he was too heavy. "(Paul) went into the bathroom and tried to pee but couldn't because he was all dried out," Yankello said. "He tried to spit and finally ended up making 135 right on the button."

Yankello rewarded Paul with a slice of pizza, and later that day, Yankello's mom treated him to a heaping plate of spaghetti and meatballs.

But the real feasting came the following evening.

Aponte was 14-9 with five knockouts. Yankello claimed Aponte's handlers argued his losses came from the hands of quality contenders and that Paul's record was built on the backs of chumps.

In lieu of responding verbally, Paul baited Aponte into eating a series of jabs and body shots from start to finish and won the 12-round contest on points to capture his first boxing championship. "Paul tortured that fucking kid," Yankello said. "(Aponte) was never even remotely the same fighter after that."

The victory netted Paul only $1,200, but he was thrilled. The IBC America's Belt was the only assurance he needed to realize bigger things were on the horizon. He wrapped it proudly around his waist and raced his motorcycle through the streets of McKees Rocks as if he had just made his first million.

Chapter 6: Coronation of a King

Paul tore through David Thomas (3-13-1) that August to win by second-round technical knockout. He improved to 22-0 with 12 knockouts and ascended to number 11 in the IBF lightweight rankings. McCauley started calling him "The Pittsburgh Kid," a tribute to Pecora and Conn, the late mentor and local champion Paul yearned to emulate. Paul continued to put in his time at the gym and believed a bout against a top-10 contender was imminent.

His October confrontation with Sam Girard, a co-feature on the Hector Camacho – Ken Signurani card at Mountaineer Casino Racetrack & Resort, and his first *ESPN2 Friday Night Fights* appearance indicated progress. Paul landed more punches than Girard (17-5-1, nine knockouts) to take each round and win a unanimous decision.

Yankello conditioned Paul to be more calculated and methodical as the caliber of competition steepened. Paul started slowly against Dezi Ford (24-20-2, eight knockouts) at Monzo's that December but picked up steam shortly after Ford opened a gnarly gash under his right eye. Paul landed jabs against Ford with increasing frequency before the ref finally stopped it in the tenth. "The longer the fight goes, the better I get," he explained.

Paul's pacing never stressed Yankello, but his fluctuating weight became an increasing concern – especially the week before Paul was tabbed to meet Rocky Martinez on January 22, 1999, as part of an *ESPN2 Friday Night Fights* telecast.

Months earlier, Martinez (29-2, 16 knockouts) had defeated Robert Nunez to capture the WBO Latino Super

CORONATION OF A KING

Lightweight Title and his ninth consecutive victory. Martinez's encounter with Paul would be staged in a tightly packed 700-seat warehouse arena behind Carmichael's Steakhouse in his home neighborhood, the West Loop section of Chicago. The challenge was daunting enough.

And then it became colossal. "Paul was 12 pounds overweight four days before weigh-ins," Yankello said. "He was already pretty damn lean, so, of course, he had to lose all the water weight."

Paul wrapped himself in plastic trash bags and shadowboxed for hours. When the strenuous sessions ended, he sweated away additional ounces in the sauna.

The deprivation paid off and Paul dipped to 135, though he was a withered shell of his former self. Through the first two rounds, he battled a motivated contender and the riotous energy of every spectator in the building. And due to his extreme weight loss, he fought his own body. He was weak, his legs were heavy, and his confidence was in shambles. "(Paul) was used to landing jabs and hearing the crowd chant, 'Spad-ee! Spad-ee!' And now he lands a couple of jabs, but the crowd is chanting, 'Rock-ee! Rock-ee!'" McCauley said. "He never had this feeling before."

Paul caught a right midway through the fifth. He stumbled back to his corner, drained and discouraged. "Angle to the sides!" Yankello directed. "Roll with the jab! Follow with a straight left! Step away from Martinez's right!"

McCauley tricked Paul into believing the bout was almost over. "There are only three rounds left," he fibbed. "This is just like an amateur fight, and you can do an amateur fight."

Paul refocused and outboxed Martinez through the next three rounds – albeit with less panache than he was typically accustomed to displaying – to strengthen his lead. When he returned to his corner with a quizzical expression at the end of the eighth, McCauley facetiously replied, "Okay, only two more now."

By that point, the ruse had served its function. Paul had recuperated and closed out rounds nine and 10 securely. The judges tallied it 97-93, 99-91, 97-94 for the visitor, and Paul survived the Windy City with his undefeated record intact.

The victory characterized his perseverance, but he bristled about the outcome and alleged Yankello gave up on him midway through the fight. Paul even claimed he could see the panic on his face between each round. "(Paul) was blaming his performance on me," Yankello said. "I was pissed because I knew it was the weight drain."

Yankello's anxiety was magnified upon learning that *ESPN2 Friday Night Fights* contributor Max Kellerman called Paul a B-level fighter on national television, adding he would never reach the upper echelon of the lightweight ranks alongside Stevie Johnson and Angel Manfredy.

The critique destroyed Paul. Acri encouraged him to consider new trainers, with Jimmy Cvetic, Angelo Dundee, and Jim McHale amongst the names mentioned as Yankello's replacement.

Despite Paul's unhappiness, McCauley saw the advantage in retaining Yankello. "Tommy worked hard as fuck," he said. "I had a shitload of respect for the time he put in, and Paul was still winning."

McHale was called to assist Yankello for Paul's March 30 bout against Eugene Johnson at Monzo's. Both trainers

CORONATION OF A KING

coached Paul to a smooth unanimous-decision win, but boxing did not generate the evening's real entertainment.

Johnson (5-10-1, three knockouts) ridiculed Paul during weigh-ins and successfully got under his skin. Squabbling between both fighters ensued through every round and became volatile after Paul was declared the victor. "Paul said something to Eugene, Eugene shoved Paul, and now they're both ready to street-fight each other," McCauley said. "I throw Eugene into the corner, and then the *whole crowd* starts fighting one another. It was crazy!"

Less than a month later, Paul's career would take an even crazier turn when IBF lightweight champion "Sugar" Shane Mosely abandoned his title and jumped to welterweight. With Mosely's sudden departure and Acri's pull, Paul catapulted from No. 11 to No. 3 in the IBF lightweight rankings and found himself on the precipice of competing for a world title.

He was euphoric. The opportunity to achieve his lifelong dream had arrived more quickly than imagined.

And he fretted it could slip right through his fingers.

Quietly, Paul left for Philadelphia to train with Marty Feldman, a former pro middleweight who had been in the corner for IBF light heavyweight champ Prince Charles Williams and middleweight contenders Dave Tiberi and Frank "The Animal" Fletcher. Feldman had Acri's stamp of approval. "I thought I was out," Yankello said. "McCauley is telling me 'Paul was falling in love with the (Feldman) guy and says he's going to be his trainer forever. But you know Paul – he changes his mind more than he changes his underwear. Don't worry – I'm not saying you're going to be gone.'"

McCauley's words proved prophetic. "Paul calls me three weeks (after leaving) and tells me he really wants to come home to train with me," Yankello continued. "I was hurt he left. All of this went down because of the shit he did with his weight. But I was also happy he was coming back."

Yankello also knew the real work was just beginning. He felt mounting pressure from Acri to groom Paul into a world champion while ensuring Paul would also make disciplined decisions with his drinking and dieting.

He began creating his game plan when it was announced Paul would meet number one ranked contender Israel "Pito" Cardona for the vacant IBF Lightweight Title on August 20, 1999, in the main event of *ESPN2 Friday Night Fights*. Under the terms of a purse bid, the higher-ranked Cardona would earn $81,125, and Paul stood to net $40,000. But Acri also negotiated to hold the bout inside The Harv – a site that was becoming Paul's home turf. "(Acri) had (first) sold the idea to Ted Arneault, the (former) CEO of Mountaineer, to put on the fight and undercard and to make it a beautiful event," Yankello said. "(Cardona) was able to be convinced to take more money and give up that backyard. It was just a good business deal all around."

Paul conversed with Pecora over the phone as they watched Cardona bully Mike Cappiello in 1996 to capture the IBO super featherweight title on *USA Tuesday Night Fights*.

Neither was impressed. "You'll beat the fuck outta this guy," Pecora uttered.

A year after defeating Cappiello, Cardona (31-2, 23 knockouts) stopped Ivan Robinson just before Robinson scored the first of his two victories over Arturo Gatti.

CORONATION OF A KING

Cardona was a bona fide banger who could electrify an entire arena with a single blow. He could also withstand abuse and lunge forward with zombie-like invulnerability.

In the same capacity, Paul, like Pecora, saw a one-dimensional bully with a concrete jawline who dared his adversaries to exchange bombs. It was a style Paul could elude and surgically dismantle. "Cardona is a power puncher, and those guys could never beat Paul," McCauley said. "As (Pecora) used to say, you could throw a handful of rice at Paul, and you still couldn't hit him."

Yankello shared McCauley's enthusiasm but knew Paul would not win if seduced by good food and late nights at the bar. He needed a break from his friends.

He needed a break from McKees Rocks.

Paul and Yankello trained for the Cardona fight at Angel's Gym in North Carolina. Over eight muggy weeks, Paul sparred against a group that included Leonard Dorin (then 9-0 with three knockouts), a fighter who, according to McCauley, possessed stronger fundamentals than Cardona. All the while, Yankello ensured Paul adhered to a stringent diet and rested well. "I babysat him," he said.

When it ended, Paul was refreshed and ready. But within days, Yankello learned his efforts were all for nothing. "I'm a new, young trainer going into a championship fight, and Acri wasn't happy," he said. "He *still* wanted a guy who had more experience."

Acri signed Jesse Reid to co-train Paul just two weeks before the fight. Reid had guided the careers of world champions Roger Mayweather, Gaby and Orlando Canizales, Bruce Curry, and Johnny Tapia. He was wise, demonstrative, and considered one of the best, but he also provided another mature influence Paul desperately craved. "Paul seemed to know a lot about me, and I already knew a lot about him because I had already been studying him for two months," Reid said. "I told Acri, 'Believe me. This kid was championship material!' I was really excited to work with him."

Yankello had completed most of Paul's training, so Reid tried to tie up any loose ends. "I only had two weeks, but because of the knowledge I had about him from before, I just added a couple of things," he said. "Paul had tremendous defense, and I wanted to help him pick up on his offense, to use his jab a little more. I wanted him to throw at least 60 punches a round."

The new arrangement put Acri's mind at ease.

It twisted Yankello's stomach into knots.

***

At 6-foot-3 and 230 pounds, McCauley cut an imposing profile. Years after competing as an amateur light heavyweight and NCAA defensive lineman for the Temple Owls, he still resembled the kind of guy you would not wish to cross in a dark alley or even a brightly lit street.

The only thing larger than his burly size and masculine persona was the expansive grin that stretched beneath his scraggly mustache. His levity lightened the tension and always helped Paul relax.

"Paul wanted a peanut butter and banana sandwich," McCauley said. "We're taking a walk, and I told him I talked to the front desk of the hotel and that he couldn't get the sandwich."

When Paul questioned him, McCauley continued spinning his yarn. "I said they have the peanut butter, the bananas, and the bread, but there are no knives in the whole building to spread the peanut butter. (The hotel staff) had to hide them because they're worried Cardona might try to slit his wrists."

Paul snickered before deadpanning, "Al, this is a serious day."

Never to be deterred, McCauley sprang back into action during the evening's undercard bouts and waved a wad of cash at Cardona and his trainer, John Cipolla.

"I'm gonna put down $2,000 right now on my guy over there," he boasted, pointing toward a thin curtain separating their adjoining dressing rooms. "Let's bet."

Paul folded over in laughter while listening to Cipolla balk at McCauley's shenanigans. The incredulity of the exchange made him feel loose.

And later that night, thanks to McCauley's jocularity, Yankello's preparation, and Reid's leadership, Paul would appear looser and more dominant than ever.

Paul figured Cardona expected him to scurry around like a frightened mouse, just as many of his past opponents had done. He imagined Cardona planned to trap him in a tight space and mete out punishment with pulverizing body shots that would weaken his legs and cut off his air. Paul sensed the need to set an early tone as he walked into The Harv and took in the earsplitting roar of 2,900 adoring fans.

Minutes later, he bobbed, weaved, zigged, and zagged through the first round, trying to keep the action away from the middle of the ring. Cardona owned a slight edge in punches thrown by the end of the second, but Paul succeeded in making it awkward for Cardona to set his feet and unleash his right.

Paul threw more jabs in the third and countered with a left that caught Cardona under his left eye. He renewed his assault in the fourth and beat Cardona at his own game, finishing the round with an 18-5 advantage in power shots.

Cardona peppered Paul's body in the fifth with alternating hooks. Kellerman credited it as Cardona's best round but noted Paul was "just boxing beautifully."

Paul answered Cardona in round six by pelting him with gorgeous-looking combos. Between shouting commands, Reid strapped on a headset and told Bob Papa and Teddy Atlas, "(Cardona) is here to win, but we're going to take his heart away from him and keep him off balance."

Cardona stalked Paul through the next four rounds in a desperate pursuit of opening a seam that would empower him to end the fight with a single strike, but Paul was too mobile. Cardona appeared aggravated, recognizing victory slipping away with each bungled attempt.

Paul exploited that frustration and went in for the kill. He circled his wobbly adversary in the eleventh and struck him like a piñata, landing multiple punches from multiple angles.

"I remember round-by-round winning every second of that fight," Paul said. "*Boom, Boom, Boom...* here he comes! *Bap, Bap, Bap*! For all the struggle and everything I went through growing up, it was to be there in that moment."

Paul closed the final round conservatively as spectators chanted his name. The final bell rang, and he jumped into Harry's welcoming arms. A lifetime of setbacks had made him more resilient, leading to a finish line Pecora always knew he would eventually cross.

Eugene Polecritti had traveled from Spokane, Washington, to watch Paul compete. ESPN2 cameras captured Pap's reaction as the scorecards were read. Once

CORONATION OF A KING

Paul was announced the winner by unanimous decision and officially declared the new IBF lightweight champion of the world, he fought back tears and beamed the smile of a doting grandfather. "I almost had a heart attack," he told the *Pittsburgh Post-Gazette*. "I didn't know what to do. I'm just so proud of him. Paul's going to be the champion for the next 10 years."

The victory also elicited a mea culpa. "I got a lot of nasty emails from Pittsburgh after I dismissed Spadafora," Kellerman said. "He didn't have such a great showing (against Martinez). I hope you guys can forgive me. I know what kind of a fight town Pittsburgh is historically, second to only New York, and Paul Spadafora – my hat's off to you. Incredible performance!"

Paul did not hold back when interviewed. "I worked real hard for this," he said. "I knew I could box this kid's ears off. I was in too good of shape. I trained my whole life for this."

He concluded, "I don't think there are too many lightweights in the world that can beat me right now."

***

If any person in Paul's crew seemed distant during the post-fight celebration, it was Yankello. After Acri hired Reid, he figured he would eventually be relieved of his duties.

But he did not foresee getting the ax that very same night. "We're in the parking lot, and everyone is happy, and then (McCauley) told me, 'We're probably going to have to let you go,'" Yankello said.

Reid respected Yankello but wanted sole control over the job he was appointed to perform. Yankello was naturally upset but understood the nature of the business and assumed the $500 check he later received in the mail was his official pink slip.

Acri was wise to imagine Reid would be a natural fit. As well as offering expert insight, he could also relate to Paul on a personal level. "I grew up with an alcoholic dad," Reid said. "He would come home, sometimes all beaten up from the bar, and my mom would be crying."

After his parents divorced, Reid and his sister moved in with their father because he had the means to care for them – though barely. By age 13, Reid drove a pick-up truck along his uncle's East Los Angeles rubbish route to help support his family. "I took steel, copper, and cardboard to the mill to collect money, or I'd go to the dump to dump off trash," he explained. "I missed a lot of school to work and make money to put on the heat in my house."

Like Paul, sports were Reid's diversion. Following standout baseball, basketball, and football seasons at La Puente High School, he played safety and second-string quarterback at Los Angeles City College and California State University, Fullerton.

But nothing enthralled Reid quite like boxing. He discovered it when he entered the Navy in 1964 and went on to amass many amateur wins at 165 pounds before qualifying for the 1968 Olympic Trials. After turning pro late at 28 years old and compiling a 5-1-2 middleweight record under the tutelage of Jackie McCoy, Reid retired early in 1970 and found his true calling as a trainer.

Working with boxers enabled Reid to build champions and teach valuable life lessons. In Acri's quest to land a venerable veteran, he had also found Paul a suitable role model. "I learned really quickly that drinking was not the way to go," Reid said. "If that was the way my dad was going to act, screw that shit. So, I never drank and never smoked. I understood Paul's mom and dad were addicts, so I understood where he was coming from."

And so did Yankello. Though they had not spoken in six weeks, Paul could not ignore his crucial role in helping him defeat Cardona, a victory the IBF would later call its "Upset of the Year." Paul's hometown threw him a parade to celebrate his world championship and erected metal signs reading, "Welcome to McKees Rocks: Home of IBF World Boxing Champion Paul Spadafora," in his honor. Pittsburgh Mayor Thomas J. Murphy even awarded Paul a gold key to the city. He was floating on cloud nine and felt like he had left Yankello at ground zero.

Paul unexpectedly popped in to visit Yankello at his gym that October. Yankello was still smarting from his callous termination but grateful to see his old friend. Without hesitation, they immersed themselves in their familiar routines, two devoted disciples of a shared religion. Paul always liked training with Yankello. He valued his opinion and missed their camaraderie. It made him re-evaluate whether he would benefit most from the influence of two trainers.

When summoned to Las Vegas later that month by Reid to prepare for a December 17 title defense against Renato Cornett, Paul made Yankello a sincere promise.

"You're going to work with me," he insisted, "and I'm gonna tell (Acri, McCauley, and Reid) tonight."

Yankello admired Paul's gumption but was not expecting any miracles. McCauley had previously stated, "A fighter should get what a fighter wants." But Paul already had a new trainer – one of the *best* in the business – and Yankello understood the trainer-to-fighter ratio is usually one-to-one for a good reason. In adding him back into the mix, Yankello knew Acri risked angering Reid and disrupting the harmony of a critical camp. It would also create friction over money.

When Yankello did not hear from Paul, he turned his attention to his other fighters.

Several weeks later, his phone rang.

"Dude, you have to come out here," Paul pleaded.

"How the fuck am I going to get out there?" Yankello said. "I got $500 for your last fight. How are you going to pay me?"

Paul's response floored him.

"I can get you back in at five percent, but Jesse gets 10."

On Thanksgiving Eve, Yankello manned the corner for Manard Reed, a promising local super lightweight who would drop his first loss to Joe Hutchinson in the main event of a small card held at St. John Arena in Steubenville, Ohio.

Later that night, he could barely contain his excitement as he sat on a red-eye bound for Las Vegas's McCarran International Airport. Paul had found a way to prevail, much as he did every time he stepped into a boxing ring, and Yankello would return to the corner of a world champion he had helped build.

And the timing was impeccable.

Had Paul not been persuasive with Acri, Yankello would have missed seeing one of the greatest boxing spectacles of his lifetime.

***

Paul trained each day at Nevada Partners, a high-end boxing facility that formerly existed near the corner of West Lake Mead and Martin Luther King Boulevard in

North Las Vegas. Yankello would hang around when the workouts ended to watch Floyd Mayweather Jr. hit the pads with his father, Floyd Sr.

Mayweather (then 22 years old with a 21-0 record and 15 knockouts) had already defended the World Boxing Council (WBC) super featherweight title four times and was *The Ring's* second-best pound-for-pound boxer. Despite the exceptional designation, he never stopped trumpeting his self-aggrandizing harangues that *he* should be ranked number one.

One afternoon, he caught sight of Paul, and the heckling got out of hand.

"Floyd (Jr.) says, 'Your boy don't want none of this,'" Yankello said. "Then he says, 'Your guy is in here whupping everyone in Vegas, but he ain't ever sparred me. I'm the best pound-for-pound fighter in the world. You guys want to get this work?'"

Paul was a week shy of his first title defense and in peak condition. Mayweather was off his regular training schedule and more than three months away from his next bout. Paul squinted at Reid and considered his position.

"I don't like the way they're talking, and I feel good about this," he said. "What do you think?"

Reid nodded and yelled across the gym, "It's got to go six rounds, not three!"

And just like that, more than five years after their meeting in a hotel elevator, two world champions bumped gloves and started to spar. Anyone fortunate enough to be inside the gym that day had front-row seats to an impromptu clash between the sport's greatest lightweights.

The anticipation was palpable, though the fireworks were not immediate. Paul and Mayweather were defensive dynamos who rarely got hit, and both executed a cautiously measured approach through the first two rounds.

Paul stepped up his intensity in the third and fourth with a beautiful blend of body punches that softened and slowed his haughty rival. Then he unleashed his right hook in the fifth and dominated the sixth, mixing jabs with well-timed uppercuts.

Seconds after the session ended, Mayweather collapsed. Battered, bloodied, and defeated, he remained on his back for several minutes. "I told (Mayweather Jr.'s) father that he was going to be sorry for talking all that shit," Reid said.

The footage was saved on Yankello's camcorder. Reid planned to use it down the road for promotional leveraging.

"Big" John Miholovich caught the action from the edge of the ring. McCauley had hired the 6-foot, 300-pound security guard to keep Paul safe during his time in Vegas.

As he watched Paul box, Miholovich realized Mayweather was the one who needed protection.

"Paul beat Floyd's body like a rug," he said. "I'd been told Mayweather always stays in shape and (challenges) guys in the gym all the time, but he really got it handed to himself that day."

Paul's parents, Annie and Silvio, smiling on their wedding day.

Paul (back row, center) and younger brother Charlie (back row, far right) enjoying sunnier days in the old neighborhood.

Paul hanging with friends (from left) Johnny Stansbury and Matty Panzino (circa 1990).

Charles "P.K." Pecora, appearing in a rare picture. Pecora was Paul's first trainer and mentor before his death.

Paul striking a fighting stance during his fledgling days as a boxer.

Paul celebrating with his mom, Annie, after dominating Israel "Pito" Cardona to win the IBF lightweight world title.

Muhammad Ali greeting Paul. Ali was one of many celebrities Paul met during his reign as Pittsburgh's "Fourth Franchise."

Paul showing off the IBF and IBC lightweight championship belts after defeating Dennis "The Menace" Holbaek at The Harv with manager Al McCauley (back left), trainer Tom Yankello (back middle), and promoter Michael Acri (back right).

Leonard "The Lion" Dorin (left) slugging it out with Paul in their bloody 2003 IBF-WBA unification bout, which ended in a draw.

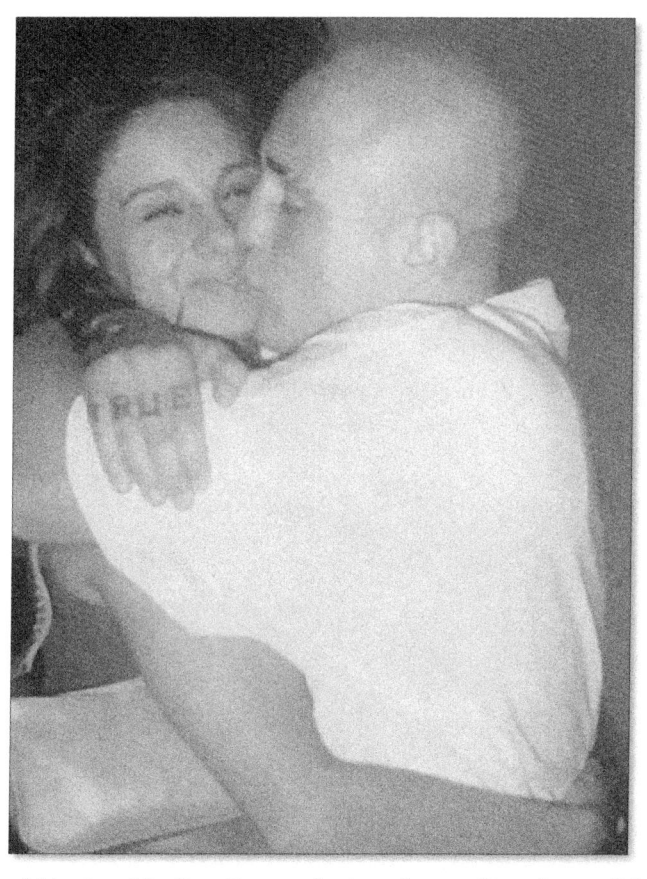

Paul kissing Nadine Russo during the earlier days of their relationship.

Paul cradling his newborn son, Geno Spadafora, at UPMC Magee-Women's Hospital.

Reporters swarming Paul at Allegheny County Courthouse after he is sentenced to seven months at Camp Hill Penitentiary and another six at Quehanna Boot Camp for the aggravated assault charges he received in the accidental shooting of Russo. (*Copyright ©, Pittsburgh Post-Gazette, 2023, all rights reserved. Reprinted with permission.*)

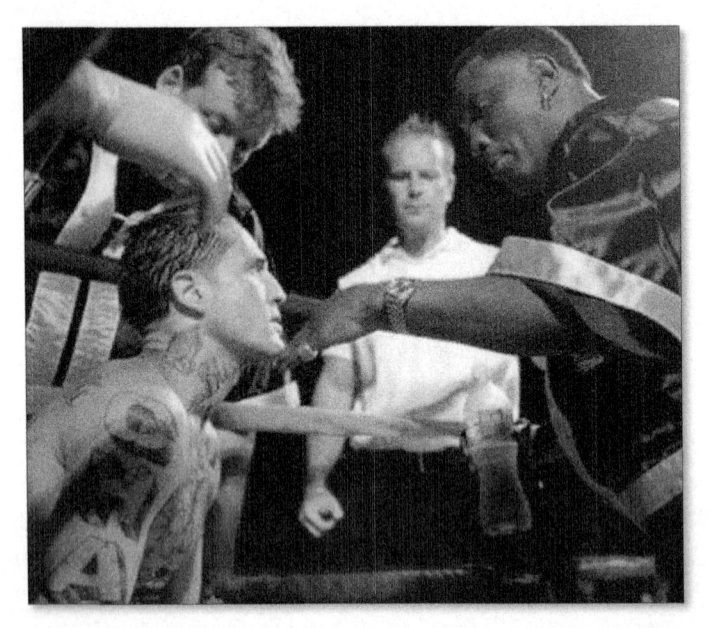

Paul absorbing pearls of wisdom from boxing megastar Pernell Whitaker between rounds. Whitaker trained Paul for three bouts during his comeback.

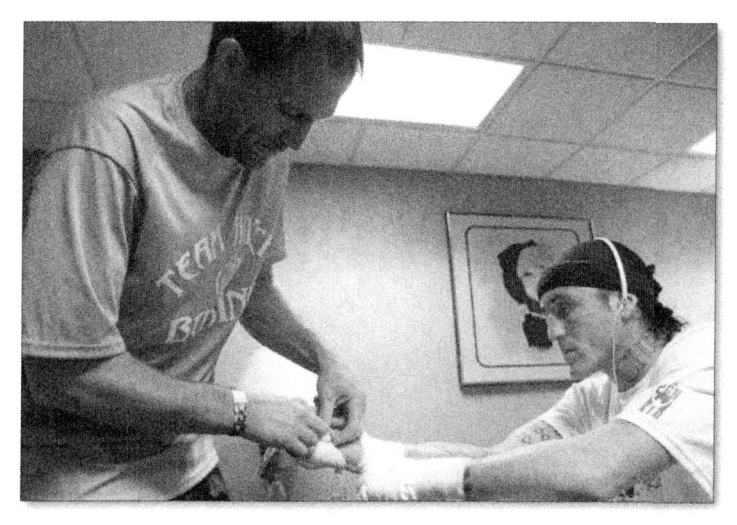

Tom Yankello taping Paul's fists before a fight. Yankello worked Paul's corner more than any other trainer.

Paul posing with Roy Jones Jr. and Geno after defeating Humberto Toledo in his first fight with TNT Promotions.

Paul stunning Solomon Egberime with a right. (Photo courtesy of 12roundsorless.com)

Paul punishing Rob Frankel before capturing the NABF super lightweight title. (Photo courtesy of 12roundsorless.com)

Paul ducking and countering against Johan "El Terrible" Perez. Despite displaying slick defense in the fight's early stages, Perez outpunched Paul to win the Interim WBA light-welterweight belt and hand Paul his first career loss. (Photo courtesy of 12roundsorless.com)

Annie, Geno, Paul, and Nadine displaying Paul's plaque after his induction into the Pennsylvania Boxing Hall of Fame. "The Pittsburgh Kid" made eight successful IBF lightweight title defenses and finished 49-1-1 with 19 knockouts.

Paul dining at one of his favorite restaurants.

Paul congratulating older brother Harry after completing the 2022 UPMC Health Plan Pittsburgh Half Marathon.

Nadine and Paul flying to Las Vegas, Paul's new home.

Paul reuniting with renowned trainer Jesse Reid (shown with Geno).

Paul visiting distant relatives during a trip to Italy.

Paul and Nadine mugging for the camera after finally getting married in the Mediterranean coastal town of Maratea, Italy.

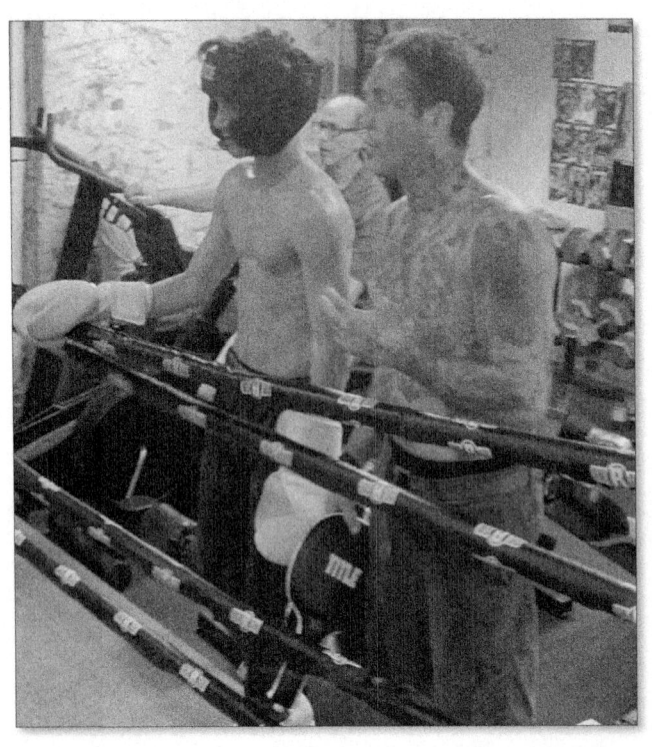

Geno learning strategy from one of boxing's best.

Chapter 7: The Fourth Franchise

The drought was finally over.

Pittsburgh was anxious to cheer on its next homegrown boxing champion, and tickets to Paul's December 17, 1999, lightweight title defense against Renato Cornett at the David L. Lawrence Convention Center were in high demand. Seated amidst the sold-out audience of 5,000-plus were retired Penguins center Mario Lemieux and Steelers Hall of Fame hopeful L.C. Greenwood. "I watched them play hockey, I watched them play football, now they come to watch me box," Paul told the *Pittsburgh Post-Gazette*. "Oh my God. This is, like, the biggest day of my life. When I heard the crowd going for me, I started getting that jive going..."

As if he needed more incentive, the bout was being televised on *ESPN2 Friday Night Fights*, and Paul was still buzzed from his Mayweather moment. He shadowboxed in the dressing room and vowed to deliver a performance no one would ever forget.

Several minutes after Cornett had entered, Paul finally paraded down the aisle. Harry helped display his brother's IBF championship belt as spectators craned their necks to catch sight of the city's newest celebrity.

Paul donned black-and-gold trunks with the initials "P.K." inscribed above the right knee. Sportswriters had already begun comparing Paul and Billy Conn, boxing's original "Pittsburgh Kid." Since the beginning, Paul knew the letters were always a nod to Pecora, a guardian angel who, in his mind, was watching down from the heavens.

And after prefight introductions, he fought as if his late mentor was whispering celestial instructions into his ear.

Paul slowed Cornett with his angled positioning in the first, then machine-gunned combos to Cornett's body in the second, at one time ringing his skull cleanly with a right. Both boxers schlepped through a sequence of elbows and headbutts in rounds four and five, but Paul pulled away in the sixth and seventh with jabs and crafty combos. "Everything I threw was hitting him," Paul said. "I was ready to go."

Cornett (30-2-1, 10 knockouts) was a former Olympian entering the zenith of a fruitful career. But as hard as he tried, the 34-year-old Australian could not gain the upper hand and fell further behind in rounds eight, nine, and 10. Paul was too persistent, too cunning, and winning almost too comfortably.

Referee Rick Steigerwald finally stopped the action in the eleventh after blood poured from cuts under Cornett's nose and left eye. Paul leaped onto a ring post and basked in the boisterous applause of his swelling fanbase.

Though not his best showing, Paul (28-0 with 13 knockouts) looked good enough to prove his Cardona victory was legit.

His performance also suggested the necessity to prioritize dollars and *sense*. The $60,000 check from his Cornett victory was the largest he had brought in, but it paled compared to the six- and seven-figure payouts he had expected to clear for a title defense.

With his popularity soaring throughout western Pennsylvania, McCauley knew more money could be made and connected Paul with personal injury attorney Mark Haak. Together, they negotiated with Pittsburgh's Iron City Brewery to participate in a campaign featuring his image on its beer cans. Paul would make several appearances at brewery-sponsored events and receive $25,000.

It was easy work, and Paul was appreciative, but no offer on the planet could muzzle his honesty. "(Iron City President) Joe Piccirilli tells Paul, 'It's really nice working with you and having your pictures on these beer cans. What do you think of all this?'" Haak said. "Paul looked at him and said, 'I don't drink this shit.'"

Haak scolded him for insulting the man signing his check, but Paul doubled down. "You mean to tell me this tastes anything different than piss?"

Preference aside, Paul could never turn away the kegs that came with the deal. After all, he still liked to drink, and the free suds generated an excuse to host several house parties.

Any alcohol, furthermore, alleviated his stress.

"I just wanted everyone to get along," Paul repeated.

***

Hostilities between Reid and Yankello reached a vituperative volume by the start of the new millennium, and Paul could no longer ignore the fact that he was being pulled in two directions. Reid agreed that Paul's defense made him tremendous but persuaded him to add more offense. Yankello hated introducing anything new that might leave Paul more susceptible to attack. He insisted his old-school defensive boxing technique needed to be perfected as it was *precisely* what made him spectacular.

Reid surmised Yankello's animus stemmed from something more personal. "Yankello was eaten up by the fact that I was brought in, but we got through it, and we were all successful," he explained. "You've got to bring in some people to help. I wasn't there to hurt anybody. If

Yankello could have looked at it differently, it could have been a lot easier."

An upcoming March 3 *ESPN2 Friday Night Fights* bout against Victoriano Sosa was another pivotal title defense, and the vitriol between his trainers became an obstacle he needed to overcome.

The solution seemed logical and was the only one Acri approved: Retain the more experienced trainer and move on from the other.

Paul laid off Yankello again that January, marking the third occasion he had done so in under a year. Yankello was never formally notified, but his dismissal was implied the morning he learned Paul and Reid had surreptitiously started another training camp without him.

Yankello had difficulty processing his release, though it was not entirely unexpected. He knew Acri always considered him a mere placeholder. Acri had always wanted an older trainer with greater prestige – which he had secured in Reid. But this time, Paul also wanted Yankello gone, believing his departure would eliminate distractions as he prepared for Sosa.

The camp ran smoothly until McCauley took a phone call from *Pittsburgh Post-Gazette* reporter Chuck Finder just days before the fight.

"(Finder) tells me Tommy says he did all the work with Paul and was his (real) trainer and that Paul wouldn't be anywhere without him," he said. "I told him, 'Tommy didn't teach Paul nothing!' and then hung up."

Atlas and Papa mentioned the exchange during the opening minute of the bout, but behind-the-scenes acrimony seemed trifling following the pandemonium that unfolded on center stage.

THE FOURTH FRANCHISE

Sosa (24-1-1, 19 knockouts) was a rising star from the Dominican Republic with a menacing right. Paul felt it during the first two rounds and struggled to return fire. He was lethargic, flummoxed, and trailing on the scorecards. Though accustomed to starting slow, something seemed discernibly off.

Paul's uneasiness gave way to terror midway through the third when Sosa started unloading heavier punches in a frenzied pursuit of a knockout. One in particular – a perfectly-timed hook – exploded like a mortar shell behind his left ear, causing him to slump to the canvas for the first time in his career as the jazzed gathering at the Turning Stone Resort & Casino in Verona, New York, rose to its feet in stunned disbelief.

"Spadafora is down, and he's hurt!" Papa yelled. "The champion is down, and he can't get up!"

"Big upset here!" Atlas cried out excitedly. "Boy, that was on the top of the head, right around the temple!"

Paul's arms went numb, and his legs turned into linguini. Woozily, he willed himself to stand up.

After Paul received clearance to continue, Sosa advanced aggressively.

"Refs going to let it go on," Papa said. "Sosa's moving in for the kill. We have a huge upset in the making! Can Sosa pull it off!"

"Look how calm he is," Atlas noted. "He just zeroes in. Look how he gets his space. He gets right in there."

"IBF lightweight champion Paul Spadafora is in deep trouble here in round three!" Papa emphasized.

Sosa hurled a fusillade of rights and lefts that caused Paul to lose balance and briefly brace his left glove against the ring floor for a second knockdown.

Paul went into survival mode. As he clinched, hugged, and attempted to tie up, he resembled a sloppy drunk trying to fend off an angry bouncer.

Sosa grinned at Paul when the bell sounded. Annie had seen enough and bulldozed through a throng of people to the nearest restroom. Her younger sister, Jackie, followed her into a stall. They wrapped their arms around each other, oblivious to the hushed whispers and furtive glances, and prayed.

Reid had no time to beseech a higher power and needed to think quickly.

"Get the ice on him!" he growled. "Paul, get your head together. You ran right into a punch! He's throwing the right hand. Spin your back leg! Are you all right?"

"Yeah."

"All right. Paul, look at me! Get yourself together now. Come on, wake up!"

Reid conjured an earlier conversation with Paul and asked, "Aren't you the same guy who once told me you'd die in the ring before giving up your title?"

The question roused Paul like a smelling salt. He let it sink in momentarily before replying, "But my legs are gone."

Reid peeked across at Sosa, who sat draped over his stool like a damp rag. Sosa's chest heaved rapidly, and he appeared punched out.

"You think you're tired? Look at your opponent!" Reid shouted. "He looks like he's dead! Let's just go one more round, and let's try to win it. If we do that, we'll go another round and try to win that one. I don't want to stop this thing because you're a much better fighter than this guy."

Paul was always a fast learner, and Sosa had pounded an essential lesson into his brain. If Paul wanted to keep

THE FOURTH FRANCHISE

winning, he could never again be provoked into fighting Sosa's fight. Instead of chasing after him and lunging with punches, he would remain calm, angle himself off, and force the heavy-handed Cuban to do the chasing. It would enable him to dictate the cadence with his defensive counterpunching.

The formula was simple, and no one could do it better.

In rounds four and five, Paul's aching body slowly achieved what his indomitable mind could conceive. He outlanded Sosa on the scorecards, and an uplifting chant disrupted Annie's mama-bear compulsion to maul Sosa. "We started to hear 'SPAD-EE! SPAD-EE!'" she said. "I returned to my seat, and he was winning."

Sosa took six, but Paul reasserted control to win rounds seven through ten. Paul was slipping punches with regularity and letting the fight come to him. As it did, he tenderized Sosa's torso with punishing body shots. "I don't know what did it, whether it was God or something else, but Sosa is falling all over the place and missing and not hitting (Paul)," Reid described. "The more Sosa tried, the harder it got for him, and all of a sudden, Paul turned it around."

Papa and Atlas were bowled over. "Spadafora has his confidence now – picking his spots, staying out of harm's way," Atlas observed. "His radar's looking pretty good. Look at his eyes – he's seeing everything. His eyes are really, really focused. He's making Sosa do what he wants to do right now, and that's Spadafora's fight."

Sosa needed to score a knockout in the twelfth, but the punches he absorbed through the bout's second half had diminished him. He raised his right glove at the very end, but Reid knew whose fist would be raised by the ref.

The judges scored it 114-112, 115-112, and 116-111 in favor of the defending champion, capping off a fistic masterpiece forged in the crucible of brutality. "This was probably the best fight I had ever been in the corner for," Reid said. "It was like Paul was allowing me to pull him through this thing, and I did. Our communication looked like magic. That was one of the greatest comebacks in boxing. It was like winning 10 world title defenses."

McCauley believed it was also symbolic of Paul's character. "Very few guys could be put into that situation and come back to win," he said. "It's by far what his life was all about."

That night, Paul returned to his hotel suite and applied ice to his swollen forehead. He fell seriously ill and was later diagnosed with a concussion at a nearby hospital. "I was throwing up everywhere," Paul said. "Sosa could fight his ass off – he ain't no joke."

What *was* somewhat laughable, he mulled, was the timing of his next camp.

Paul found himself on a flight for Texas less than a month later to prepare for a May 6 bout against Mike Griffith. Reid had arranged for them to train at Houston's Main Street Gym alongside Lou Savarese, a heavyweight contender gearing up for a June collision with Mike Tyson.

The opportunity initially seemed too great to pass up. Paul was offered $150,000 – his largest purse ever. The fight would take place at Mellon Arena in the heart of downtown Pittsburgh and be shown on the debut of HBO's *KO Nation*. Acri also believed Griffith (23-6, nine knockouts) was another stepping stone that could lead to contracts against more bankable juggernauts like Stevie

THE FOURTH FRANCHISE

Johnson, Ivan Robinson, Jose Luis Castillo, and Floyd Mayweather Jr.

Griffith was a carpenter-by-day fighting out of Loraine, Ohio. Aptly called "The Hammer," he was expected to give Paul a solid workout and nothing more.

Nonetheless, Paul worried he was being set up for failure.

Hard work had always been the antecedent to any advancement in Paul's career. He trained like a madman at the gym, open till close, and often had to be told to leave. And that did not change in Houston. Reid challenged Paul with a mob of talented Mexican fighters, and Paul did everything he was told.

But through it all, he was never up to the task. "Sosa fucked me up pretty bad," Paul said. "Then I flew out to Texas and had to lose a lot of weight because I had gone up to 170 pounds. I shouldn't have been anywhere near a gym! Harry should have told Mike I'm not going to let my brother take this fight."

With the wheels already set in motion, Paul sweated profusely and crash-dieted to near collapse. He entered Mellon Arena and confronted a scrappy underdog who planned on trading his toolbelt for Paul's glitzier IBF title belt.

Griffith's determination was unmistakable right away. He tracked Paul around the ring and landed more punches to take two of the first three rounds.

But then the bout took an unimagined turn when unintended headbutts (one from Griffith in the third and another from Paul in the fourth) opened gashes above the right eyes of both fighters, obligating their cutmen to play critical roles in determining the outcome.

Griffith's wound was gaping, and Mike Laquatra's meticulous attempts to cork it became increasingly arduous. Paul's laceration was less severe and a much easier assignment for Delio. Even though it would later warrant eight stitches at the ER, Delio controlled it with his homemade *grease* (a mix of Vaseline, coagulant, and other ingredients).

Delio's handiwork enabled Paul to focus. He gained a slight edge by landing several jabs on Griffith's incision and connecting with several body shots in rounds five, seven, eight, and 10.

As Laquatra became less productive in preventing the seepage, ringside physician Dr. Lawrence Biskin called the fight before the start of the eleventh, and the judges awarded Paul a controversial majority decision.

His thirtieth consecutive victory might only have been possible because Delio kept him looking clean and pretty. "(Griffith) wasn't in Paul's class, technically, but he was very strong," McCauley said. "Paul had a concussion after the Sosa fight, and he came back too soon. We were getting close to making really big money, but this fight was too close. This was the only mistake (Acri) made, and he didn't ever make mistakes."

Paul agonized over the stale effort and spent weeks re-evaluating his decision to retain Reid over Yankello. Reid commandeered respect in boxing because he knew how to build champions. He also treated Paul like a son. But Reid's time was also stretched thin because he trained several world champions in Vegas, and Paul had barely endured his previous two fights. "He blamed Jesse and wanted Tommy back," McCauley said. "I was the last one who had wanted Tommy to go, but I also didn't want him back after all of the bullshit that went down."

THE FOURTH FRANCHISE

Neither did Acri, who begrudgingly released Reid and re-signed Yankello to a two-bout contract that would be re-visited if his boxer remained unbeaten. "The Griffith fight was a terrible fight – the worst I ever fought," Paul said. "I made money, was on HBO, started to feel like a franchise, and had a great following, but started to not be like a real fighter anymore."

He added, "After I fought Griffith and looked like that, my addiction to alcohol became overwhelming."

***

Though won by the thinnest of margins, Paul's third successful title defense only added to his growing mystique.

Nearby Monessen native Michael Moorer generated interest after scoring a majority decision over Evander Holyfield to win the lineal IBF and World Boxing Association (WBA) heavyweight belts in 1994, but he trained in Detroit and claimed the Motor City as his real home.

As Paul's nickname intimated, there was no ambiguity over his geographical allegiance. "The Pittsburgh Kid" *was* Pittsburgh, and Yinzers loved him because he boxed with a blue-collar grittiness that epitomized his hardscrabble upbringing. Fans rejoiced after each hard-earned victory, and neighborhood boxing gyms swelled to capacity with pint-sized pugs looking to lob their best punches. The *Pittsburgh Post-Gazette* and *Pittsburgh Tribune-Review* reserved larger patches of real estate for the Spadafora beat alongside its regular coverage of the Steelers, Pirates, and Penguins.

Regionally, Paul resuscitated a pastime that had flatlined a half-century earlier. "When done right, boxing was cool, incisive, and strategic," said *Post-Gazette* sportswriter Chuck Finder. "That's what made the early (old-school) fights fun, and Spaddy brought that back."

With fame came newfound stardom that enabled Paul to live out an existence he had only seen in movies. He signed scores of autographs, posed for pictures, and made new friends everywhere he went. He skipped lines at nightclubs and accepted a bottomless well of free drinks. Following last call, he would continue the party at his favorite after-hours spots until the morning sun crept over the horizon.

Women took notice of Paul and, like booze, became another hedonistic vice. His dimpled smile, flirtatious charm, and bad-boy persona fueled a revolving door of female companionship. The dalliances, writ large, distracted him from his disappointment over the Griffith bout.

One encounter, unexpectedly, led to something meaningful.

Paul approached Crystal Connor at a pizza shop on Liberty Avenue. They talked while he took swigs from a 40-ounce bottle of malt liquor. He sneaked glimpses at Connor's pretty eyes. He walked her home, and they went on their first date soon after.

Connor was different from the other women Paul had encountered. She was quiet, and her conservative personality grounded him.

Alternatively, Paul's drinking could not be tamed by anyone, and the late nights impeded his ability to earn. Haak knew he had a problem on his hands that July when Paul cost himself a peanut butter promotion with Giant Eagle, a local supermarket chain. "The contact guy tells

THE FOURTH FRANCHISE

me, 'Deals off! Your client is a thug! He beat up my breadman!'"

It was discovered later that Paul's crime was only one of complicity. He and a pal had wandered behind the grocery in Robinson Township after an evening of heavy drinking and urinated on the side of a bread truck. When the driver got confrontational, Paul's buddy leveled him with an overhand right. "Then (Paul) tells me they put the man in the back seat of his truck," Haak divulged.

Paul pleaded guilty to disorderly conduct and paid a $300 fine, but his involvement cost him an agreement worth $40,000.

Yankello pushed Paul back into the gym for his September 9 nontitle matchup against Rodney Jones. Despite his flawless record, Paul had lost his winning swagger, and Yankello knew he would never find it at the bottom of a Guinness. "Paul was drinking, and then I got him to stop," Yankello said. "I was putting the pieces together after he had that performance against Griffith."

Paul regulated his eating and lost the necessary pounds to make weight, but he still felt incomplete. Against Yankello's wishes, he asked Reid to fly into town to aid them on the day of the bout. Though Paul still faulted Reid for his performance against Griffith, he missed Reid's presence. "(Paul) knew he could always come to me and talk about boxing and get good information," Reid said. "He always knew I had his best interest at heart."

With both trainers in tow, Paul returned to The Harv – the site of his commanding world title conquest a year earlier – and promised a thrilling encore.

Jones (23-0, 10 knockouts) had never faced quality opposition. Paul was a noticeable jump in height and skill, so the Arkansas fighter lowered his 5-foot-4 stance to literally and figuratively pull the IBF champ down to his level.

The strategy was nothing more than a mere annoyance to Paul. He outclassed Jones to win each round – knocking him down twice in the seventh and once in the eighth – to snag an easy 10-round unanimous decision.

The competition was inferior, but Paul needed to once again feel in control. He needed to hear the crowd chant his name. And most importantly, he needed to remind himself about the importance of respecting a sport that had given him so much.

After a two-week respite, Yankello eased Paul into a new training camp, leading to a December 16 mandatory title defense against Billy Irwin. Paul was in a good place, and Yankello was committed to maintaining his momentum.

Paul anteed up by hiring Sam Rulli, a western Pennsylvania Golden Gloves boxing champ turned personal nutritionist. Rulli eliminated salt, alcohol, and late-night snacking and increased Paul's metabolism with a six-meal-a-day, protein-rich diet. He even permitted Paul to move in with him, and they bunked together that November when they moved the camp to Fayetteville, North Carolina.

The experiment appeared to work initially. Paul made 135 pounds for his pre-fight weigh-in and felt relatively good. But he rewarded himself gluttonously that day and into the next by binge-eating his favorite foods and ballooned to 153 pounds before returning to the David L. Lawrence Convention Center that evening.

Irwin (34-3, 24 knockouts) fought out of Niagara Falls, Ontario, and had represented Canada in the 1992 Summer Olympics. He was riding a hot streak of 11 straight knockouts under the auspices of a vicious left. His first appearance on HBO's *KO Nation* was to be the pinnacle of his accomplishments, so Paul expected him to come out swinging hard.

Oddly enough, it never happened. Irwin held his gloves cautiously high from the get-go and rarely threw jabs. The few times he did, Paul slid away and countered. Paul was the aggressor with the speedier mitts, and as the bout progressed, he was the fighter setting the pace.

Irwin's traveling fanbase briefly came to life in the fifth when he lashed Paul with successive power punches.

That was the same instant they met Paul's mom. "Annie turned around with her knees on the back of the chair, a box of Cannolis tucked under her arm, and screamed, 'Which one of you motherfuckers wants a piece of me!'" Haak said. "There were a hundred Canadians that were like, '*Holy Fuck!*'"

Paul did not need outside help from his family. He showed signs of his old, dominant, defensive self and was barely grazed. "I felt like (Spadafora) made me miss," Irwin told the *Pittsburgh Post-Gazette.* "He made me look wild and sloppy. No excuses. I got out-stroked."

By the end, Paul had landed 147 punches to Irwin's 70 and won unanimously. "Irwin was never able to lay a glove on Paul," Yankello said. "It was like a cakewalk. Irwin had good blocking defense, but he didn't have enough head movement to narrow the distance on Paul, he didn't have a good enough jab, and his feet weren't the best either. Paul could have banged Irwin up, but from the two fights he had previously, he was a little gun-shy to be completely open-ended with his offense. That scar tissue from those two fights stopped him from boxing as offensively as he could have. He still had that defense and used that angling, and Irwin didn't stand a chance."

***

Paul was 32-0 (with 14 knockouts) and had just deposited another $75,000 into his checking account, but he still coveted a bigger-named challenger and a bigger payday.

Before looking toward 2001, he needed to address a more serious concern.

Paul's body went into shock the week following his Irwin victory. He landed in the hospital as a result of gaining 30 pounds in three days after depriving his body of sodium for more than three months. Doctors hooked Paul to an IV drip to treat severe dehydration. Once discharged, McCauley instructed him to rest while Acri worked on his next fight.

The advice seemed sensible but made Yankello anxious for obvious reasons.

With additional time off and plenty of cash to spend, Paul reconnected with his McKees Rocks roots. He met up with his brother, Charlie, at their favorite watering holes and bought rounds for everyone in the room. He added more tattoos and expanded his growing collection of sneakers. That February, he closed on a two-bedroom ranch house on Ella Street below the McKees Rocks Bridge. He even enhanced the property with a bricked-in bar, game room, and gated car port, and Harry installed an elaborate concrete sidewalk across the front. "It was by far the best home in McKees Rocks," McCauley said.

Paul decided he was ready to work again as the bills piled up that spring. He was the undefeated IBF lightweight champion of the world and expected to secure

THE FOURTH FRANCHISE

a marquee fight against a legitimate contender. And he reasonably assumed it would pay top dollar.

Upon learning his May 9 title defense against Joel Perez would be part of a benefit card with proceeds supporting the newly formed Professional Boxers Assistance Foundation, he realized he would have to wait.

Perez (31-4-2, 18 knockouts) was reeling after losing a unanimous decision to a middling talent named John "The Macho Midget" Bailey. "(Perez) wasn't the kinda guy I was dreaming about fighting like a Stevie Johnson or César Bazán," Paul said. "I didn't understand it. How do you go to this after looking like I did against Cardona and then proving yourself against Sosa? You shouldn't be going backward after that."

Either way, the 12-round main event would still air on the inaugural *ESPN2 Tuesday Night Fights* telecast, and it was another paycheck and title defense he could ill afford to turn down. The bout would also be held under the I.C. Light Amphitheater tent along the south shore of the Monongahela River, denoting Pittsburgh's first outdoor contest since Jersey Joe Walcott stopped Ezzard Charles at Forbes Field in 1951.

The historical gravitas went unnoticed by Paul for personal reasons.

Polecritti, 74, was battling terminal cancer and had returned from the West Coast to be closer to family, and Paul knew it would likely be his last opportunity to see him box.

Pap's presence always gave Paul an extra spring in his step and snap in his jab. It provided the intangible boost he had been seeking since his days at St. Ignatius when he painstakingly scanned the stands for Silvio during his youth basketball games before turning away in disappointment. Pap was a free spirit who lived in various parts of the country, but he was always there for his grandson when it mattered most.

That night, it underscored Paul's determination to put on a dazzling show. He abandoned his defensive playbook in the opening round and revved up the 3,500 gathering with some run-and-gun offense. In preference to ducking and dodging, he squared up and attacked. Paul suffered punishment – most notably a bloody nose in the second – but also connected on several combos to build a lead.

Paul knocked Perez off his feet with a stealthy left in the fourth. Perez hurriedly stood back up, but the IBF champ was on him from that point forward. Paul clobbered Perez with two lefts in the sixth and opened a cut above his left eye with a hard right in the eighth. "I was trying to take it to another level," Paul told the *Pittsburgh Tribune-Review*. "I didn't want to save anything for the dressing room. If I wanted to make this kid chase me and let the crowd go to sleep, I could do that. I want to keep the title, but I also want to live out my dream and have fun out there."

This revealed itself in the later rounds. Paul walloped Perez with a left in the tenth and goaded him to toss his best punches in the eleventh. Paul's vintage defense manifested itself only in spurts. He mostly left himself wide open, caught some heavy shots, and landed a few of his own.

Paul toyed with Perez in the twelfth as the seconds ticked away. He later slapped on an Iron City cap after pitching a near-perfect shutout on the scorecards to win by unanimous decision.

THE FOURTH FRANCHISE

As friends and TV cameras swarmed him, Paul's thoughts shifted to his grandfather. The victories were always sweeter when he was watching in person.

He wrapped up a post-fight interview, hugged his Pap, and continued to the dressing room.

Six weeks later, Paul said goodbye to him at his funeral.

***

Pap's death hit Paul harder than any he had experienced. He tried to work through the malaise during training camp for his August 14 nontitle fight against Charles Tschorniawsky. He hit the pads during the day and worked a pen each evening. "I was having trouble, so I wrote," Paul said. "I got my feelings out. It was just bad."
As he completed each journal page, he almost forgot his upcoming opponent was quite dangerous.

Tschorniawsky (20-3-1, 11 knockouts) went by "Chucky T" to avoid the hassle of spelling and pronouncing his last name. He competed out of Philadelphia and had won the Pennsylvania Golden Gloves Championship at 112 pounds the same year Paul captured it at 132. He was a plucky fighter with a nasty right. He was also reeling from an upset defeat against Larry O'Shields (16-10-1, seven knockouts) and desperate to rebound with a win over an IBF champion.

With both Paul and Tschorniawsky moving from lightweight to junior welterweight, Paul counted on owning the advantage in power.

The night of the fight, a slightly heavier Paul Spadafora walked down the aisle in a robe stitched with the words "RIP, 1927-2001, True Love" to honor his grandfather.

He followed up by unleashing his pent-up emotion before 4,100 rowdy fans at The Harv in a tribute his Pap would have appreciated.

Tschorniawsky burst out of the gate and rocked Paul with a wicked combination. He hoped to engage Paul in a slugfest.

Paul responded with a jab that bloodied Tschorniawsky's nose and then went to work on Tschorniawsky's body and head through the next several rounds. He fought with great tenacity.

To those who knew about Polecritti's passing, he also appeared inspired.

Tschorniawsky was up for the challenge. After getting belted with a left cross in the fifth, he moved in closer and delivered several headshots. He even walked to Paul's corner at the end of the round and taunted him to continue.

Paul opened a cut under Tschorniawsky's right eye in the sixth round and outpunched him through the seventh and eighth, again inciting Tschorniawsky to follow Paul after the bell. He demanded Paul's best.

And Tschorniawsky would get it throughout the final two rounds.

Paul split open a new laceration under Tschorniawsky's left eye in the ninth and, in the tenth, landed a blow that sent his mouthpiece airborne.

Chucky "T" could have actually stood for "Tough," but he was outmatched. The judges agreed, and Paul rolled to 34-0 with another unanimous decision. "It was a good fight, but I beat the living fuck outta him," Paul gloated. "Chucky was the perfect style for me. Again, it was like target practice."

THE FOURTH FRANCHISE

As the wins continued to mount and the target on his *own* back grew, Paul could not begin to realize that his biggest challenges would not await him inside the ropes.

Chapter 8: In the Confluence of Chaos

Paul threw himself into training before his bouts and drank himself into a stupor after. Following his Tschorniawsky win, he began adding ecstasy into his repertoire. Paul chased each tablet with alcohol, met up with his brother Charlie, and let his troubles slip into oblivion. "Between fights, I was fucked up every day, doing everything wrong under the sun," he said.

Paul's world became even more complicated that fall when Connor revealed she was expecting. Though he loved being an uncle to Harry's son, Paul questioned whether he was in a good place to care for a baby when he struggled to care for himself. He also wondered how differently his childhood might have been had his own father shown any interest. "I never wanted to have a kid until I had my life right," Paul admitted. "I wanted my house to be paid and my money to be right – so I tried to do it the right way. I figured I could put (Connor) in a place and be with her and be a good dad."

Connor's news coincided fortuitously with negotiations to match Paul against Angel Manfredy in a co-featured main event on HBO's *Boxing After Dark*.

Manfredy (39-5-1, 29 knockouts) of Gary, Ind., was the IBF lightweight division's number-one ranked mandatory challenger. Despite losses to Floyd Mayweather Jr., Diego Corrales, and Stevie Johnson, he muscled out impressive technical knockouts over Arturo Gatti and Jorge Paez, a unanimous decision over Ivan Robinson, and a split-decision victory over Julio Diaz.

His proclivity for theatrics, however, made him particularly entertaining.

IN THE CONFLUENCE OF CHAOS

For most of his career, Manfredy went by the handle "El Diablo" (The Devil) and wore a latex Satan mask into each fight. The costume perfectly embodied a maniacal fighter who punched like a man possessed and a feral hellraiser who partied like there was no tomorrow.

In several instances, there nearly was not. Excessive drinking led to a dozen car accidents and a three-day cocaine binge that pushed Manfredy to the brink of suicide. He claimed a spiritual awakening moved him in that moment, and he dedicated his life to religion.

The new, clean, sober Angel changed his alias to "Got Jesus" but retained his demonic left.

Paul was undergoing his own conversion. He was about to become a dad and wanted to eradicate drinking and drugs permanently. It was a process that could be facilitated more readily inside a gym as he trained for a fight – preferably against a high-level boxer who would earn him enough money to put his girlfriend and the new baby in a respectable home.

In Manfredy, Paul saw an opening to check off these boxes, and he jumped into camp that October before a deal was even inked.

Paul had gained 35 pounds since his last bout and deduced the early start would give him ample time to shed the weight. He hit the pads, skipped rope, shadowboxed, and went through the perfunctory routines that usually did the job. But progress was slow. When it was finally announced in December that the fight would be moved to March 9, 2002, Paul had only shrunk to 160.

Despite his frustration, Paul continued to grind. He sparred Lamar Murphy, a skilled boxer whom Manfredy had just beaten by unanimous decision, and fine-tuned his technique with each session. The extra mass melted away, but Paul was famished as the fight neared and debated whether an eventual bump to a heavier division was unavoidable.

That consideration, Paul knew, would need to be tabled for another day. Manfredy was a top-shelf fighter who, like Israel Cardona, disregarded Paul's talent. He told reporters he would soon take Paul's IBF lightweight belt and even promised a knockout.

Paul never sweated Manfredy's power but did worry about feeling depleted. The extreme dieting diminished his strength, and he did not want to perform listlessly in a mammoth title defense.

Before the fighters made their ring walks at Duquesne University's A. J. Palumbo Center, the HBO team of Jim Lampley, Emanuel Steward, and Larry Merchant discussed the significance of the matchup. "Through all the years with Manfredy, through his cycles of ups and downs and reinventing himself, of winning and losing and winning, of turning to the devil then turning to God, one thing has been constant; he always comes with his best effort," Merchant said. "That best effort hasn't been good enough to beat the very best fighters, but it has been good enough to beat the next best fighters. He is a walking, breathing, fighting, battling litmus test for the local favorite tonight. We'll find out where Spadafora stands."

Manfredy appeared driven from the opening bell to ensure it would not be upright. He charged at Paul like an ornery bull and threw long, looping hooks. Though three inches shorter, Manfredy owned an abnormal two-inch reach advantage that helped him land twice as many punches. He won the first, although the only damage – a bulging welt above Paul's left eye – was inflicted by a headbutt.

IN THE CONFLUENCE OF CHAOS

Paul bobbed and weaved through the next several rounds and threw off Manfredy's timing. He landed a swift left that moved Manfredy back in the third, which incited Merchant to affirm, "That had some pop on it."

As the fight proceeded, Paul became more relaxed. He moved around the ring like a poised matador, often making Manfredy miss. His angling progressively became razor-sharp, his movement more elusive, and his counterpunching more prominently effective. Several four- and five-punch combos drew a chorus of "oohs" and "aahs" and helped Paul build a solid lead on the scorecards.

"Spadafora is actually punching harder than Manfredy, which is a big mistake on Manfredy's part," Steward observed. "Manfredy is throwing right hands with no power."

"What Spadafora is showing is that his footwork and understanding of his body and angles are just nifty enough to take away some of Manfredy's power," Lampley said. "You don't easily get clean shots against Spadafora."

Co-trainer Sam Colonna advised Manfredy to push in closer. He wanted his boxer to bang away – it was his only shot. "Don't let him play with you!" he hollered. "You have to knock this guy out! You understand! You have to get serious!"

Manfredy cracked a hard right into Paul's chest in the tenth. The thud was loud enough to induce a groan from the pro-Spadafora crowd and was Manfredy's most brutal punch of the night.

Still, it was too little, too late. Manfredy continued to hunt and pursue in the final rounds, but Paul was well in front on points. He played it safe until the finish, and all three judges scored it 115-113 to give him another unanimous decision.

Merchant compared Paul's boxing approach to a baseball team that knows how to get on base and score efficiently. "They have speed, they go from first to third, they sacrifice, they do all the right things," he described. "They don't win with three-run home runs."

As the HBO cameras panned in, Paul (35-0, 14 knockouts) summarized his success in general terms. "I'm very confident about who I am and about my style as a boxer, and I feel that I'm a younger champion and I'm bound to get better. I just gotta change my habits up on the outside life, and I think I'll be around here for a long time."

***

The Manfredy fight netted Paul $500,000 – the largest check of his career. At 26, he was wealthier than he could have ever envisioned and thankful for a chance to finally rest.

Acri called a week later with other plans. Paul's performance opened many doors, and the one Acri was choosing to walk through required his southpaw to begin training immediately for a summer matchup against WBO titlist Arturo Grigorian.

"I was motherfuckin' just in camp for six months!" Paul scoffed. "Why do I gotta go back this very second? I just fought!"

Paul had been hurried into camps too quickly in the past – even once after suffering a severe concussion – and it seemed as if history was repeating itself. He could not deal with the idea of toiling through another minute in a humid gym while depriving himself of nourishment.

IN THE CONFLUENCE OF CHAOS

When Acri refused to budge, Paul rebelled by using the one thing he did control – his body. After hanging up, he swallowed a handful of ecstasy tablets and slammed 10 bottles of malt liquor. "My mom rushed me to the hospital because of all these pills," Paul said. "I threw up maybe 30 times. I was dying in the car."

Paul got his stomach pumped before returning home a few days later. His team recognized his breakdown as a cry for help and gave him space. Acri would tell the media Paul was being treated for a stomach ulcer and the Grigorian bout would be postponed. "Mike got all paranoid about how to present it, but what did it really matter," Paul said. "The (overdose) was the real reason the fight fell through."

But it also freed up an opportunity to reconnect with a more familiar foe.

Paul caught a Vegas-bound flight that April to watch Mayweather battle Jose Luis Castillo at the MGM Grand for the vacant WBC and *The Ring* magazine's lightweight titles. He alleged Mayweather had been making threats against him, which implied stories of their acclaimed sparring session had been making the rounds. Paul prayed his audacious adversary would coast past Castillo.

A win would preserve his aspiration of challenging him in a certified bout to prove that their exhibition was indeed no fluke.

Paul ran into Mayweather at the casino on the day of his fight and even wished him luck.

"(Mayweather) told Paul, 'Don't worry, you're next!'" claimed Johnny Stansbury, a childhood friend who joined Paul on the trip. "So Paul said, 'Please, let me be next!' as we were walking away, and Mayweather yelled, 'Where you going? I'm talking to you! I'll run right through you, white boy!'"

Another member of Paul's entourage countered, "He already beat you!" goading Mayweather to allegedly grumble, "It's way different under those lights."

Paul was relieved Mayweather took enough rounds to earn a slim decision that night and remain undefeated, but he could not move past Mayweather's tirade. "No one can run right through me because of my heart," Paul said. "I'm just not going to let that ever happen."

When Paul was at the top of his boxing game, he believed he was invincible. And by the summer of 2002, Paul felt that way everywhere he went. He partied like a rock star, and his nights were blurred with the help of drinking buddies who wanted the celebration to last for eternity. "We were young, having a good time, (Paul) was the champ, and we were on top of the world because we felt like one of us had made it," Brandon Cercone said.

The revelry almost made Paul forget he was about to become a father.

Paul's rapport with Connor had been deteriorating for months, but after she gave birth to a baby girl that July, he revisited his original idea of settling down to co-parent a child while he worked on his sobriety. In the short term, he planned to put his house on the market and move in with Connor while they looked for a new place in a safer neighborhood. He imagined his new daughter, Gianna "Spit" Spadafora, would keep him levelheaded as he evolved into a sensible adult.

It eventually became unfeasible, nonetheless, to ignore the reality of their dilemma. Paul and Connor shared in the merriment of bringing another life into the world, but they were different people, and their relationship had run its course.

Paul became depressed, knowing he would struggle to see Gianna regularly, but reasoned he could always return to the same rituals that helped him dull any pain.

***

Nadine Russo noticed Paul's wild streak while serving drinks at Lucky Charms, a popular bar in Pittsburgh's South Side neighborhood. She also detected his sense of entitlement when he asked for a bottle of Captain Morgan without reaching for a wallet.

"That will be $100," Nadine said.

Paul looked confused, prompting her to tease, "What, you can't afford it?"

He shrugged and sheepishly replied, "At least I know you aren't using me for anything."

People jockeyed for Paul's attention – it came with being a world boxing champion. But Nadine was most captivated by his eccentric personality.

She ran into Paul on several occasions over the next month. Each time, he hit her with a ridiculous tale or outlandish idea. One afternoon, he swam up to her raft at a wave pool and bragged about the mini gym and steam room he had just installed in his McKees Rocks home.

"Why would you ever do that?" she asked him, snickering over the absurdity of enhancing a residence in a low-income community with opulent amenities.

When Paul told her he had stolen the idea from a rap artist who did the same thing on an episode of *MTV Cribs*, Nadine was flabbergasted. "Immediately, I had this 'I have to save Paul!' mentality," she said.

Paul enjoyed making Nadine giggle. He was also drawn to her luminescent smile, flowing brown hair, and voluptuous frame. In his mind, she gave new meaning to the term *knockout*. "Nadine was the prettiest girl I'd ever seen," he professed.

And in many ways, she was very much like him.

Nadine began smoking marijuana and cutting class at age 14. Teachers at South Hills Middle School alerted Child Youth Services, and she was sent to Gannondale, a former residential behavioral center in Erie that Nadine called "a nunnery for adolescent girls."

The following year, after returning to Mt. Alvernia Catholic School, Nadine alleged she was tricked into snorting heroin by an older teenager who would also impregnate her. When Nadine's mother, Barbara, discovered her apartment had been robbed by the same teen a few days later, she called CYS, and Nadine was mandated by court order to live at Auberle Girls Group Home.

Nadine later escaped and went on the run. Once she was found and returned, a judge ordered her to Danville Detention Center. She was released on house arrest as her due date approached and emancipated from the juvenile justice system after giving birth to a daughter, Brianna.

As she matured, Nadine owned up to the mistakes of her youth. She passed her GED exam and enrolled in childhood education classes at the Community College of Allegheny County. She would bear a second daughter, Margo, from another relationship a year later and try to get her life on track.

Nadine looked into Paul's eyes and imagined they were kindred spirits destined for one another. She also knew he was working through unresolved issues with a woman who had just made him a new dad and kept a conservative distance, oblivious to problems that were far more detrimental.

The Manfredy victory had made Paul rich, and he lived like a king. He lavished buddies with gold Rolexes. He paid his mother's debts and bought Harry a $25,000 Bobcat to help with his new construction business. That August, he posted bail for a friend and suspected drug dealer named "Teardrop," who was arrested at his home during a narcotics sweep. And then there was his 2003 Hummer H2, a $55,000 purchase partially financed through his brand-new Cadillac Escalade trade-in. "What happened to Paul was the same phenomenon that plagues people when they win the lottery – their lives start to get destroyed, and they sabotage their success," said boxing historian Douglas Cavanaugh. "They don't know what to do with all of this money; they don't know how to manage it. Paul was a street kid from McKees Rocks. He's got all of this money and all of this time off (between bouts). What's he supposed to do – of course, he's going to spend it."

Until it was nearly gone.

Paul's bank ledger incurred substantial damage by the fall, and his waistline had become bloated. Ravenous overeating and regular blackouts pointed to the obvious – he needed to resume boxing. When Acri informed Paul he would fight Dennis Holbaek in a unification title bout at The Harve on November 10 for a $200,000 purse, he quickly purged the toxins and excess body fat through rigorous workouts that left him feeling beaten and fatigued.

He had no other choice. Holbaek was not Mayweather, but the Danish boxer was still the IBC world champion and owner of a 43-1 record with 22 knockouts. Paul had managed to get past Manfredy with a subpar showing but knew another one would result in his first loss. Marvin Hagler famously mentioned how difficult it was for fighters to wake up and complete roadwork at 5 a.m. when they had been sleeping in silk sheets. Paul's linens could be lathered in vomit on any given morning following a late-night bender. Hard living kept him from reaching his optimal ability, and he struggled to curb his destructive appetites between fights.

Paul felt engorged but reassured upon discovering he only needed to cut 20 pounds – 10 less than he had grown accustomed to losing in his three previous camps. He made weight the day before the fight feeling good and presumed his improved strength would help him against Holbaek.

Later, to his chagrin, it did nothing. Paul looked rustier than usual in the first round and got tagged with a hard right in the waning seconds of the second to fall behind early.

He readjusted by the third and landed some hooks and uppercuts. "That was a better round – much better!" Reid boomed. "You're starting to put your hands together. Keep working your hands, don't forget your jab. Be busy. You be the boss. Don't worry what he's got – he ain't got shit! Keep them hands working, all right! You looked real good that round. Get a little bit busier now!"

Reid pantomimed with his fists. "I want everything off, every move. *BING-BING*! Just let him keep seeing those hands, keep moving. *BING-BING*!"

But the momentum seesawed back to Holbaek. He clocked Paul with a left in the fourth that opened a small incision below his right eye, then staggered him with an overhand right. "(Holbaek) hurt me," Paul confessed. "It woke me the fuck up real quick."

Per usual, it was exactly what he needed.

Paul worked his jab with precision and landed hooks to Holbaek's body in the fifth, sixth, and seventh. He enlivened 4,500 fans in the eighth with a rapid five-punch combo and a sturdy left to Holbaek's mouth.

"Beautiful round, Paul," Reid bellowed. "Now that's how to fight! You're the boss! You're the boss! I want to back this guy up and run him out of here. You hear me? He wants to come in and grab you! I want both hands in that gut, and then you come back to the head!"

Paul weakened Holbaek with forceful body shots. By the end of the twelfth, he knew he had done enough to add Holbaek's IBC belt to his wardrobe. But after the judges made his unanimous decision official, Paul wore the expression of someone who had just been defeated. He graded his performance a "D" and would tell the *Pittsburgh Post-Gazette,* "I felt that in the first four, five rounds, I couldn't get off. I was really sluggish. I was really slow. I didn't feel good. I didn't feel right."

The following day, Paul would return to the lifestyle that was mostly to blame.

"I used to be like everyone else and say if only (Paul) did the right thing, he'd be unstoppable at 135," Yankello said. "But he wasn't doing the right thing, and there comes a time when you have to say it is what it is, you can't control it, so you just have to make the most out of it."

***

Nadine often met up with Paul during the Holbaek camp, and they became a couple by winter. One of the first things they did together was use cocaine. "I wasn't a drug addict but was used to being introduced to that kinda stuff," she said. "All of Paul's friends partied, but at the time, Paul didn't even know how to sniff drugs."

After doing a few lines, Paul broke down. "He was crying and so mad at himself like it was the worst thing he had ever done," Nadine said. "I was like, 'Oh no! I've just ruined his life!'"

Once the shock wore off, Paul continued using, and his Holbaek revenue provided the funds needed to feed his new habit. They would also need to cover for his mom, who had begun using coke regularly. Paul did not realize how severe Annie's addiction was until the night he and Nadine visited a North Side pub called Peanutz to pay off her dealer. "The guy told me she owed $1,400, and I was like, 'Motherfucker, are you serious!'" he said. "My mom ain't there, and I'm mad as hell, so I wanted to stay and drink."

Nadine, conversely, was anxious to leave. They were in a sketchy neighborhood past 2 a.m., and Paul's flirtatious overtures with a female barback made her irritable. She followed him down a flight of stairs to a small, dilapidated bathroom, and they argued.

A large black male who saw Paul's transaction with the dealer interrupted them. He towered over Paul as he stood at the urinal, blocking the doorway, and ordered him to hand over his drugs.

The conversation became unsettling when Paul told him he was not carrying anything.

"Then you're going to give me all of your money, or I'm going to fuck you in front of your girl," the man replied.

Paul pulled a .38 caliber pistol from his waistband and aimed it at the stranger's chest. Tears dribbled down his jawline as he thought about pulling the trigger, essentially ending the lives of two people.

"The guy was getting really loud – you could tell he didn't want any problems anymore," Nadine said. "People from the bar heard the noise and came down the stairs, so I grabbed the gun from Paul, and we ran out."

Paul grasped any involvement with cocaine could lead to danger, but it did not prevent him from snorting even more.

Reid wanted to push Paul into another camp that January as Acri negotiated a potential Spadafora–Mayweather IBF–WBC unification match at Madison Square Garden. When dialogue dissolved due to discrepancies over the proposed disbursement (a $2.7 million – $300,000 split that favored Mayweather), he took matters into his own hands and brought Paul to his Costa Mesa gym in Orange County, California, as they awaited his next fight. Reid altered Paul's training regimen by adding tire drills to augment his power and a rotating bag to enhance his counterpunching. He also challenged Paul with a cadre of West Coast sparring partners at Freddie Roach's Wild Card Gym in Hollywood.

Most importantly, Reid kept Paul sober and clean, and it enabled Paul to make rational decisions.

His next one would be easy.

Paul elected to continue his training with Yankello at Buzz Garnic Jr.'s Round 2 boxing gym in Coal Center, Pennsylvania, upon learning he would meet two-time Romanian Olympic bronze medalist and WBA lightweight champion Leonard "The Lion" Dorin in an IBF-WBA title unification bout scheduled for May 17, 2003.

Nestled within the wilderness of the Allegheny Mountains, Garnic's compound offered fresh air and rugged seclusion to boxers priming for big fights. Dorin (21-0 with seven knockouts) presented Paul with his biggest. Although his punches lacked zip, Dorin was prone to throw many. He averaged over a hundred per round in his 2002 title defense against Raul Balbi. And like Gatti, Dorin was willing to take multiple shots to the face and bleed out profusely to win.

Paul remembered training with Dorin before defeating Cardona several years earlier. He stood just 5-foot-4 but fought with a giant heart.

If Paul ever wished to challenge Mayweather, he would need to get past Dorin convincingly. He visualized his strategy as he jogged the scenic trails along the Monongahela River. He sparred with IBF junior lightweight champ Carlos Hernandez (another busy fighter in the vein of Dorin) and former WBO bantamweight title holder Alfred Kotay. He felt at peace and told reporters he was amidst the best camp of his career.

And its therapeutic benefits stretched beyond sport.

Paul's commitment toward self-improvement one month would often be invalidated by his careless detachment the next. His training in the woods allowed him to start over and do things correctly. He ate healthy meals. He fished in a stream, rented movies, and took long walks. He wrote in his journal. He attended Sunday mass at the local Catholic church.

Then, after reconnecting with his spiritual center, he broadened his scope. Paul sold his McKees Rocks bachelor pad and purchased a place closer to Yankello's gym in Ambridge. He made plans to settle down with

IN THE CONFLUENCE OF CHAOS

Nadine and start a family. He arranged to invest his Dorin income (totaling $400,000) into a stable future. He was adamant about changing for the better.

Dorin's team, meanwhile, was interested in a different change – specifically in the way the Pennsylvania State Athletic Commission selects its ringside judges. The appointment of two Americans (Patrick Russell of California and Gary Merritt of Indiana, both from the IBF) and just one foreigner (Guillermo Perez Pineda of Panama and the WBA) drew their sternest condemnation. They also protested the addition of Philadelphia referee Rudy Battle and considered withdrawing Dorin altogether.

According to the *Pittsburgh Post-Gazette*, representatives from the Montreal-based Interbox organization voiced dissatisfaction during a press conference at Pittsburgh Brewing's Ober Brau Haus in Lawrenceville the day before the bout over what they considered a conspicuous advantage for Paul. "It came down to one neutral judge [Perez], two American judges, and one American official for an American fighter in his home country," said Interbox consultant Don Majeski. "I feel on Saturday night, I don't know who will win the decision, but I know who will win the fight."

A random voice from the crowd hollered, "Then why fight?"

Majeski said of Dorin, "He's a better man than I am."

Paul reaped the benefits of boxing in front of a local crowd many times over but chided talks of collusion. He knew a decisive victory would be the only way to end the commotion. Once again, he would get his chance in another main event on HBO's *Boxing After Dark*. Merchant speculated beforehand whether Paul could finally silence the cynics. "Nationally, (Paul) is viewed as some kind of local phenomenon, like a strange beer they haven't tasted," he said. "The supposition is he is a protective fighter who hasn't faced the stiffest competition, that he has been protected by fighting at home, and also that he is a pure boxer in an age when there are very few fans who are purists. Locally, they wonder maybe that's all true, but especially they feel we haven't had a serious fighter come out of Pittsburgh in two-thirds of a century. Could this kid be the one? They can't believe it. Maybe he can change perceptions tonight."

Paul would do just that but in a different way. Those acquainted with his defensive aptitude would have predicted him to absorb very few punches against Dorin. Save for a near career-altering mistake against Sosa, he had practically mastered the pugilistic artform of hitting and not getting hit.

But that night, before some 5,200 spectators at the University of Pittsburgh's Petersen Events Center, Paul veered from the beaten path, just as he had done against Perez. Minutes after entering the arena to R. Kelly's "I Believe I Can Fly," Paul threw caution to the wind and met Dorin head-on. He surprisingly directed less attention to his angling and did not juke away from Dorin's predictable onslaught of rights and lefts. Paul came back at him with two uppercuts but landed only a single jab.

In place of returning to the long-established technique that had made him a world champion, Paul stuck with the abnormal tactic through the next two rounds. Dorin threw a high frequency of punches. Some missed wildly, but some connected with authority. Paul countered with body shots from close range and opened a wound above Dorin's right eye in the third.

IN THE CONFLUENCE OF CHAOS

"This is not new for Dorin," Lampley said. "Dorin cuts and bleeds in most fights."

"He said, 'I bleed to win,'" Steward reminded. "He's got the bleeding part down."

Dorin attempted to return the favor against Paul with two rights. Paul shook his head defiantly as if to indicate he was unscathed before Dorin opened a grotesque gash above Paul's left eye with an accidental headbutt.

Reid applied globs of salve after the bell, but the crimson wound was pronouncedly visible as Dorin continued throwing rights and lefts in the fourth. He challenged Paul to brawl, and Paul accepted his invite each time. By the end of the round, Paul had landed only 81 punches on the night to Dorin's 143. "Spadafora is not used to fighting at this pace, and he's not used to getting hit as much," Merchant remarked. "You wonder whether he can sustain whatever plan he has or whether he's going to have to change back to his more natural style."

"I don't think he can change now," Steward said. "I think he's gotten into a pattern or rhythm, and the flow of the fight is not going to change that much."

Paul ate several rights in the fifth but returned hooks and uppercuts to Dorin's body to take the round. His trainers trusted the output would be enough to generate a spark in a fight Dorin was controlling.

"You box like that, and you will win every fucking round, you understand me?" Yankello said.

"All right, I'm gonna box all night," Paul answered.

"That's right!" Reid said.

"You box all night!" Yankello and McCauley yelled in unison.

"I can do it… I can do it," Paul repeated.

Dorin smashed Paul with a right in the sixth. By the fight's midway point, Paul had already encountered more punches than in any 12-round bout.

He remained undeterred and stuck with his approach. He chopped at Dorin's ribs and abdomen through the next two rounds, expecting to wear him down. "When I was hitting (Dorin) to the body, he was making these girl-like sounds," Paul said. "I thought he was going to quit because I was killing him."

The numbers on the scorecards, however, told a different story. Dorin's short and stout punches were squeezing between Paul's guard and making contact with his face. After the eighth, Paul had only won two rounds. Reid continued to plug the swollen abrasion above Paul's left eye and worked earnestly to seal a new cut above his right.

Paul blamed himself for letting the fight get out of hand and knew he needed to dig deeper than ever to preserve a reputation he was not ready to surrender.

In the ninth, Paul finally unveiled a desperate, back-against-the-wall urgency that produced conclusive results. He circled Dorin with partially obstructed sight and fired four-punch combos with conviction. He moved fluidly and made it difficult for Dorin to make contact.

"Three more rounds like that, and you're the champ!" Yankello shouted.

Dorin returned to his overhand right in the tenth while Paul pounded at Dorin's stomach and ribs. Paul appeared to be heating up, and his fanbase was coming to life.

Both boxers tapped gloves after the bell in a display of mutual respect, just as they had done following every round.

IN THE CONFLUENCE OF CHAOS

Dorin's trainer, Stephan Larouche, sensed a momentum shift and demanded focus. "Stop being the nice guy, okay!" Larouche stressed. "This guy wants you dead, not alive! Stop being the nice guy, all right! No more friends now. It's over!"

Yankello, likewise, demanded more production from Paul. "We need speed right now, combinations, four and five punches at a time!" he urged.

Added McCauley, "We need 100 punches this round, baby!"

Paul would not hit that tally, but he did take the eleventh with a blistering hook that ripped into the flesh above Dorin's left eye. Dorin bounced on the balls of his feet and displayed energy, but Paul landed more shots.

Larouche did his best to inspire Dorin heading into the final stanza. "Give us some speed, all right! Give us some speed!" he commanded. "Get to the body! For all your family, for all of Romania!"

Across the ring, McCauley was equivalently emphatic. "This is your whole life, baby! Your whole life!"

Paul whipped the crowd into hysteria midway through the twelfth with a four-punch combo that re-opened the contusion above Dorin's right eye. Dorin moved in close, seemingly indifferent to the blood that cascaded down his cheeks, and launched more rights and lefts of his own. It was a battle of wills, powered by pride, adrenaline, and unflappable determination, and neither fighter backed down.

When the final bell rang, the tired combatants embraced. Paul was swollen and scraped, and Dorin was caked in gore. The bout had been a tense-and-taut tit-for-tat that would be tricky to evaluate, but Paul assumed his command in the final rounds would be just enough to squeeze out a nail-biter.

Judge Pineda agreed, giving Paul the edge at 115-114, but Russell's 115-113 ruling for Dorin and Merritt's 114-114 stalemate resulted in a draw, and both fighters retained the belts they carried into The Pete.

Paul slumped his shoulders over the ropes after the decision was announced. "I thought I won the fight," he told Merchant. "(Dorin's camp) made a big deal about coming into our hometown, and I guess the managers and their promotor did a good job because (the judges) came into my hometown, and they were biased against me. Who do you think won the fight, Lar? And you be truthful."

"I'd call it a draw," Merchant said candidly.

Paul smirked, replying, "You wasn't watching what I was watching when I was fighting."

When pressed to elaborate, Paul explained, "I thought I needed to win the last two rounds just to win unanimous. The last round, I thought I won big enough to close the show. I fought like a true champion, stood in front of him, threw a lot of punches. They gave it a draw. When I got the draw, I didn't even want the fight. I want to run it back as soon as possible. Let's run it back! Let's try to unify this! Please, Leonard Dorin's people! Please, Mike Acri! Let's run it back and see what we can do from here!"

After receiving medical attention, Dorin summarized his feelings during a post-bout press conference. "I met a real warrior," he said. "That's why it was a great night for all of us. I think the people were happy because they came to see a fight, and it was a great fight."

***

IN THE CONFLUENCE OF CHAOS

Despite shoddy efforts in several title defenses, Paul had always found ways to persevere and preserve his pristine record. At 36-0-1, it finally had a stain. The draw hung around his career like a noose that could ostensibly choke out any shot of ever fighting Mayweather.

It also incentivized him to make sweeping changes.

Paul started with the scale. He decided he was finished being an emaciated 135-pound fighter and that June relinquished his IBF and IBC lightweight titles to compete in the more manageable 140-pound junior welterweight class. "It was real hard, but whenever you can't make the weight, it's a happy decision," Paul told Kevin Gorman of the *Pittsburgh Tribune-Review*. "As much as you don't want to give up the title – you either want someone to beat you for it or retire with it – I can't do that to my health."

His second adjustment was much more complicated.

Paul had remained tightlipped about Reid and Yankello in recent bouts, hoping their relationship would mend on its own. Reid's commitment to several other world champions kept him on the West Coast and away from Yankello for extended periods, so they rarely found themselves in the same city, let alone the same gym. But the Dorin fight reignited their original dispute over strategy. Yankello was miffed that Reid had emboldened Paul to move in close and experiment with his offense, believing Paul would have won had he boxed more defensively from the perimeter.

Reid was attempting to make Paul marketable for HBO, which could open the door to bigger paydays. Yankello strove to keep Paul moving down the path Pecora had placed him on years earlier. "With Jesse, I needed a father figure in my life because I never had one," Paul said. "He gave me security, confidence. Tommy would get mad and then say everything is fine, and everything wasn't fine. Tommy would say Jesse was taking me down the wrong path, saying he wasn't getting the best outta me, that I'm not supposed to ever sit (in front of an opponent) like that."

Paul knew their dissonance would plague him forever and finally canned them both. He convinced himself their dismissal was a long time coming and looked forward to a new beginning.

And initially, it felt gratifying. Paul was thrilled to hear Emanuel Stewart was being considered as his new trainer. Acri also left the door open for a Dorin rematch while he continued chasing more tantalizing options like Gatti.

But once the gravity of the shake-up was fully digested, Paul became distraught over the departures of two men he considered family. Reid was a living legend in the boxing world. Kellerman ballyhooed Yankello as one of boxing's top trainers during a 2002 *Friday Night Fights* telecast. Both men were stabilizing influences. Without them, Paul knew he would fall into the same patterns that invariably put his life in peril.

By then, Paul had returned to drinking with a motley mix of leeches, sycophants, drug dealers, and addicts. His Dorin earnings made him a millionaire, and he spent it carelessly. "(Paul) bought everyone in the bar drinks, and that always brought us unwanted attention," Nadine said. "We'd drive home in the middle of the night, and crackheads on the bridge would scream 'PAUL!' He'd pull over and give them money. He always gave everyone money. If we went to Benihanas, Paul would give the chef money. People at that restaurant loved him because he would hand them hundred-dollar bills."

IN THE CONFLUENCE OF CHAOS

Paul balanced the bedlam with moments of sensibility. He put a down payment on a three-bedroom home in Moon Township, a wealthier Pittsburgh suburb. He even discussed marriage and the possibility of children with Nadine. But as promising as Paul could make the future sound, Nadine grew concerned about him surviving the present. "He would start drinking, then sometimes he'd start crying, then he'd want to go find his mom, then he would hate himself and want to die – it was all of these different emotions," she said. "I understood Paul went through a lot as a kid. But when he drank, it wasn't like he was having a good time, and then he would just drink and drink and drink until he couldn't drink anymore. When I would look at him, I would see a broken child, and I would just try to talk to him, especially when he would be really upset."

Nadine would also chat with Acri when things would get unmanageable. "I was definitely the buzz kill and was always dry-snitching on him," she explained. "I would be on the phone with Mike Acri and tell him he's drinking. We were always trying to watch Paul. He was like a bad little kid."

And as she would come to learn, bad behavior could quickly turn deadly.

In the early morning of Sunday, October 26, 2003, Nadine found herself bleeding to death from a gunshot wound. The newspapers would later confirm what she already knew.

Paul Spadafora, the former IBF lightweight champion and her boyfriend, had pulled the trigger.

Chapter 9: Loaded and Dangerous

Nadine collapsed on a concrete slab under the dim, fluorescent lighting of a gas station in McKees Rocks, covered in blood and laboring to breathe. She had been shot in the chest by Paul's revolver.

A customer from one of the pumps applied pressure to the wound as police and paramedics arrived. Nadine clung to life. Paul knelt at her side. He was angry, discombobulated, and pronouncedly drunk as he slurred his testimony. He became more lucid in the back of a squad car as an ambulance rushed Nadine to Allegheny General Hospital. "Cops were calling me a scumbag," he told *Sports Illustrated*. "All of these people wanted to judge me, and they had no idea what really happened."

Paul wrestled with the details himself. He knew he had been arrested two days earlier and charged with public intoxication and open lewdness after he was caught urinating at a downtown Pittsburgh intersection. He spent a night in Allegheny County Jail, posted bail in the morning, met up with Nadine, took ecstasy, and continued drinking.

The litany of ill-omened choices continued late into the evening. Paul hazily remembers hopping around to various bars. There was lots of bickering. Nadine wanted to go home, but he wanted to keep going. "Paul would always say, 'We'll leave after this beer,' and then he'd come back with a new one and say, 'Just one more,'" Nadine said. "He's talking to all these random people, and I'm getting bitchier and bitchier."

Somewhere along the way, a friend passed Paul the handgun. Paul claimed he needed it for protection amidst swirling rumors that a group of men was conspiring to abduct him for ransom.

Rather than taking the news as a cue to leave, he stuffed the weapon into his waistband and ordered another round.

Paul blacked out before closing down one of his favorite dives in McKees Rocks. Afterward, he insisted on driving to Molly-O's, a Sheraden pub owned by a close friend who occasionally opened her doors outside business hours. Nadine begged Paul to call it a night as he sped away, but she could not reason with him. "(Paul) pulled over on the side of the road to pee, and I jumped out and told him I wasn't going with him," she explained. "He gets back in (the SUV) and leaves me there. I had to hitchhike up the hill to where he was going."

Nadine found Paul wandering the sidewalk when she caught up to him, indicating he had been refused access to the closed bar.

Paul had forgotten he had left Nadine stranded moments earlier as he hugged her and asked, "Where you been, babe?"

Nadine ushered Paul into his vehicle's passenger seat and began the commute back to their new house. She was exhausted but thankful that their horrible outing seemed to be ending.

And utterly unaware that the real nightmare was only beginning.

While passing back through McKees Rocks, Nadine decided to buy an iced tea. As she approached the entrance to a British Petroleum (BP), she absentmindedly crossed Paul's Hummer over a median strip, slashing both front tires.

Her heart raced as they jumped out to assess the damage. Paul became combative but for irrational reasons. "He wasn't even that mad at me about it," Nadine said. "Paul still just wanted to go get fucked up – that was his whole mission."

And he would not be stopped. After shoving Nadine into the passenger's seat and guiding the vehicle into a parking spot, Paul slid onto the asphalt, slammed the door, and stomped up the street. Remembering the earlier threat against his safety, he pulled out his revolver and gripped it loosely as Nadine gave chase. She pleaded with him to return, but Paul was too committed to finding his next sip of alcohol.

"I guess I'm just driving home with two flat tires then!" she screamed before changing direction and heading back toward the Hummer.

In the same millisecond that Paul sloppily twisted around to grumble a response, it happened – an involuntary twitch of the finger, a flicker of light, a horrific accident that sent a bullet through Nadine's purse and back before exiting her right breast.

He watched in horror as Nadine staggered toward the pumps. Acting on impulse, he chucked the gun away from himself in disgust and frantically chased her. Harry Nicoletti, an off-duty corrections officer buying coffee, caught Nadine as she fell. She gasped for air and writhed in pain as Nicoletti tried to stop the bleeding, initially inducing Paul to threaten violence. "He yelled at the guy to stop touching my boobs," Nadine recalled. "That's how messed up he was."

According to the *Pittsburgh Tribune-Review*, Nicoletti said Paul complied with Nicoletti's request to dial 911 on Nadine's cell phone. When paramedics showed up,

LOADED AND DANGEROUS

Nadine had already lost four units of blood. She wearily asked an EMT if she would die but was more concerned about Paul. "I told the person helping me that regardless of what happens, she had to tell (Paul) to get out of jail and be with me because he is my only family," Nadine said. "He was on ecstasy and drinking two days in a row. I know he didn't mean to shoot me."

Paul had enough awareness to realize cops would see things differently. He was taken in for questioning and quickly released after telling detectives Nadine had been shot by one of two assailants in an unsuccessful attempt to steal her purse. The account was porous and reeked of desperation, but it bought him time.

Later that morning, hours after Paul's Hummer had been impounded, police gathered witness testimonies from Nicoletti and Mike Fabianne, a cashier at the gas station. Fabianne had seen Paul and Nadine argue after Nadine had driven over the median. Nicoletti had watched Nadine follow Paul down a sidewalk toward a nearby oak tree. Although neither witness had viewed the shooting, neither had observed anyone else in the area.

Once investigators recovered a .38 Smith and Wesson containing four live rounds and a spent cartridge under the same tree Nicoletti had described, they secured a warrant for Paul's arrest on the charges of attempted homicide, aggravated assault, reckless endangerment to another person, and illegal possession of a firearm.

But their window had already closed.

"I got a call that morning from (managing financier) Jimmy Rizzo saying, 'Al, Paul shot Nadine. He's on the run,'" McCauley said. "I go to (Paul's) house. He's gone. We can't find him anywhere."

***

The bullet from Paul's gun had missed penetrating vital organs by centimeters and made a clean exit. Following several hours of emergency surgery, Nadine's condition was upgraded from critical to stable.

A harrowing catastrophe had been miraculously averted, but Paul was uninformed of Nadine's improvement and naturally presumed the worst. He had blood on his hands and planned to leave town right away. He arranged to hide with a friend in New Jersey until he plotted his next move.

Before going on the lam, Paul decided to drown his depression in one more beer bottle. McCauley was grateful for the delay. He found Paul that afternoon less than 20 miles away at Bear's Inn, a working-class tavern in Harwick. "At 1:30 (p.m.), news breaks in with 'Paul Spadafora is being sought for shooting his girlfriend, Nadine Russo.'" McCauley said. "Everyone turns to look at him, and he just shrugs his shoulders."

McCauley alerted Paul that Nadine would recover from her injuries. The update unleashed a flood of emotions. "I told (Paul) if he runs now, he'll be running for the rest of his life," McCauley said.

Paul was supposed to be moving into training camp with Steward that day in what was anticipated to be a new and exciting chapter. He instead returned home and waited for the police to take him to jail. He was detained and released the following day after posting $50,000 bail. A night court judge ruled that Paul had to submit himself to drug and alcohol counseling and have no contact with Nadine while awaiting trial.

Nadine emerged from her mental fog around that time, and memories of the weekend slowly resurfaced. She panicked in her hospital bed as she considered the potential repercussions of Paul's actions. "When Harry came to visit me, I tried to rip the tubes out of my throat and was so worried about him," she said.

More explicitly, Nadine was petrified about what would become of Paul. The situation looked bleak, and she knew the facts would be met with rigid skepticism. Paul would be painted as a savage who wanted her dead. She assumed he would be locked up for years, maybe decades, and was afraid that their relationship would never survive the separation.

Nadine was discharged from the hospital a few days later and stayed with her father. According to reports from the *Pittsburgh Tribune-Review* and *Pittsburgh Post-Gazette*, she attended Paul's pretrial hearing on November 10 but remained outside the courtroom because she was too scared to testify. On the other side of the wall, Nicoletti presented evidence that indicated Paul as the shooter. He alleged that he asked Nadine if a boyfriend had shot her, telling the judge, "She just slurred the word 'Yeah' in a moaning-type voice," before admitting that she never did give him a name.

Defense attorney William Difenderfer dismissed Nadine's moans as the ramblings of a person under extreme distress and argued it "defied logic" that she would ever want Paul to ride with her in the ambulance had he fired the weapon.

District Judge Mary Ann Cercone believed the evidence was sufficient to proceed with the trial and reiterated that Paul was to stay away from Nadine as a condition of his bail.

***

After nearly killing his girlfriend, Paul was more than ready to accept his problem with drinking and drugs and seized upon the opportunity to heal. He attended Alcoholics Anonymous and Narcotics Anonymous meetings daily. He ducked away to Detroit for two months to train with Steward that winter before flying to California to rejoin Reid, a man who provided the calming presence he always needed. Paul relied on Reid's support weeks into his visit after hearing Delio, 81, had died of a heart attack in Pittsburgh while driving home from the gym.

Paul's longtime cutman had been a critical contributor to his success. He even reminded him of his Pap.

As Paul mourned Delio's passing, he felt unmotivated to make his April 29 debut in the 140-pound junior welterweight division. His opponent – Ruben Galvan – was unheralded, and the venue – The Hilton Garden Inn at Southpointe – was unremarkable. Additionally, he stood to make only $15,000, a mere pittance next to the compensation he collected in larger arenas.

The details were as unfulfilling to Paul as a pint of O'Douls, but he swallowed his pride and attempted to treat his ballroom bout against Galvan (20-4-2, nine knockouts) like another title fight. Buoyed later by news that Nadine was pregnant, he planned to christen the occasion with a thunderous knockout.

Despite feeling more powerful with the added mass at welterweight, Paul looked every bit like the boxer who had competed at lightweight that night. He was technically superior, but he was never able to hurt Galvan. He would take another trouble-free unanimous decision, yet he was again irked.

LOADED AND DANGEROUS

Reid helped Paul recalibrate for a July 17 matchup against Costa Rica's Francisco Campos (18-0-1, 10 knockouts). It would be held on the South Side at the Chevrolet Amphitheater and pay $25,000, but Paul was soured by the fact that it would not be televised.

Campos briefly knocked Paul from his high horse in the second round by opening a cut above his right eye. Paul squinted through the stream of blood and flexed his superiority in the middle and later rounds with combos that caused Campos's left eye to swell. After tearing open a gash above Campos's right eye in the tenth, the referee called it and awarded Paul his first technical knockout since his 1999 title-defense victory over Renato Cornett.

But Paul remained displeased. Even though he was 38-0-1 with 15 knockouts, his career sputtered on shaky ground for the first time in years.

The only constant was Nadine. She remained by his side through thick and thin. It was them against the world, and Paul liked the notion of keeping it that way forever. He proposed to Nadine that summer with a 3.8-karat diamond, and she eagerly accepted.

Nadine knew the conditions for marriage were less than ideal. Paul was due in court that October, and she expected him to go away for a long time. She also knew the relationship was improving. She ogled her gaudy ring and believed she deserved to be happy with Paul after everything they had been through.

And then, in the blink of a blissful eye, she was reminded that her new fiancé remained a slave to the mind-altering substances that impeded any progress when his friends started bringing him cocaine and 40-ounce bottles of malt liquor. Before long, Paul fell back into the unhinged routines that almost got her killed less than a year earlier.

Paul was charged with disorderly conduct, public drunkenness, and reckless endangerment to another person that September after he pulled the parking brake of his Cadillac CTS while Nadine was driving it. Allegheny County Common Pleas Judge Jeffrey Manning placed Paul under house arrest and ordered him to wear an ankle bracelet that limited his outside freedom.

It was another wake-up call, and Nadine felt demeaned when it went unheeded. Matters worsened when Paul initiated a secret liaison with a female resident at the halfway house. And when Nadine was away, he would also see Connor.

Nadine put on a brave face and tried to ride out the storm, uneasily hoping things would return to normal after she finally bore him a child. After Paul's trial was delayed a month to permit authorities additional time to inspect DNA evidence on the confiscated gun and then another to enable him to undergo elbow surgery, she began to count down the minutes until her first contraction.

When it coincidentally arrived on her birthday – December 1, 2004 – and doctors at UPMC Magee-Women's Hospital delivered a healthy baby boy, she smiled with pride as Paul cradled his son and gazed into his eyes for hours. They named him Geno after Paul's Pap. "I loved it," Paul said with emotion. "It was one of the best days of my life."

It would soon be followed by one of his worst.

Paul failed a random drug test that detected cocaine in his system less than a week after leaving the hospital and two weeks before his twice-rescheduled court appearance.

LOADED AND DANGEROUS

Judge Manning issued an arrest warrant for violating the terms of his bond.

Nadine buckled Geno into his car seat and drove Paul to Allegheny County Courthouse. Hours later, he was handed a two-month jail sentence.

As Paul walked to his cell, he could only curse about his plight, knowing substance abuse was the impetus behind his every foolish move.

Luckily, through legal counsel, Paul made a wise one at his December 17 hearing when he *admitted* to accidentally shooting Nadine and pled guilty to only aggravated assault and a weapons charge. With sparse evidence and Nadine's continued refusal to testify, the district attorney's office dropped its attempted homicide and reckless endangerment indictments. "Difenderfer was good at negotiating pleas, and he got Paul a great result," Mark Haak said.

Despite the victory, the addict in Paul was still running the show. He badgered Nadine to sneak drugs into the prison for him. Her refusal made him more determined to achieve his aim, no matter how hazardous the risk.

Paul rolled the dice only two days before his trial after being granted a morning furlough to get "a procedure" done on his teeth. He visited his dentist and drug dealer and returned to Camp Hill in under two hours with a mouthful of gold veneers and a sandwich baggie filled with gifts for his fellow inmates. "I smuggled coke up my ass, along with (Percocet), (Xanax), and cigarettes," he said. "I did what I had to do."

Paul would maintain that mindset at his sentencing on February 23, 2005. Prosecutors had withdrawn the weapons allegation, but Paul understood the assault charge carried up to five years in prison.

His voice trembled as he addressed Judge Manning. "I want to say I'm very sorry for what happened that night," Paul said. "If you can just give me this little chance, I'll make you so proud. I'll make this whole city proud."

Nadine also pleaded for clemency, stating, "Paul don't know nothing but drinking and boxing."

Much to their surprise, Judge Manning responded with a benevolent verdict: Seven months at Camp Hill Penitentiary, followed by another six at Quehanna Boot Camp in Karthaus, Pennsylvania.

Once again, Paul had wiggled out of another tight spot, just as he had done throughout several climactic title defenses. In a short period, he could resume boxing and work with Nadine toward putting the trauma of their night behind them.

Escaping the drama of his past year would be a taller order. Hours after sentencing, Connor informed reporters that she was three-and-a-half months pregnant with another of his children. "August 9, it's due," she said. "Paul knows it's his kid. I'm not sure what he tells Nadine, but we can get a DNA test. Nadine just wants to believe they're just this picture-perfect couple, and she's the only one who Paul loves. But what's she gonna do when I pop his child out on August 9?"

***

Nadine wanted to forgive Paul and blame his infidelity on drinking, and she trusted Camp Hill would provide structure and help facilitate his recovery. She was identified as Paul's victim and prohibited from visiting, but nothing would prevent her from seeing her fiancé – not after everything they had experienced.

LOADED AND DANGEROUS

She used a friend's driver's license and made monthly trips with Geno unnoticed. Each face-to-face interaction was reassuring. Paul consumed three square meals daily and pumped iron four nights a week. He benefited from a regular sleeping schedule. He wrote in his "Books to God" journals and sent letters to his family.

The experience was cathartic for Paul, and Nadine could sense he was doing well. "I had a lot of leeway because I was a (former) champ," Paul said. "It was a lot like boxing camp."

Nadine's contact with Paul was more restricted at Quehanna, so she opted to play it safe. She stopped visiting and making phone calls, knowing it would jeopardize his parole, but found imaginative ways to communicate. "I'd send letters to him using a friend's address in the third person, writing things like 'Hey, I saw Nadine today, and she's doing well,' because (Quehanna staff) would read his mail."

Quehanna's military-style atmosphere enabled Paul to thrive. He set records with the boot camp's physical tests and returned to fighting shape. He also benefitted from the program's drug and alcohol rehabilitation component. He became more disciplined, almost as if he was preparing for another bout. "Drill sergeants went hard – their goal was to break you," he said. "It was torture, but I did great there and kind of liked it."

As his April release date approached, Paul looked out his window and thought about Nadine and Geno. They had a home in the suburbs and an opportunity to lead a good life.

His mind wandered further as he reflected on his connection to Connor, who had given birth to his second daughter, Giovanna, during his confinement at Camp Hill.

Paul's past child support payments to his first daughter, Gianna, had been sporadic. He wanted good relationships with both girls and realized he needed to improve.

All of it required monumental change. Paul had blown through most of his money, and his ability to provide for his expanding family would hinge upon his ability to rebuild his career. He would first need to take control of his sobriety. To do so, he would need to stay busy at all costs. "The addiction piece with boxing is really unique because there is no standard on and off-season," explained Dr. Adam Gallenberg, a licensed sports psychologist based in Minneapolis. "When training camp starts on a certain date, that's when (the fighter) is on. But when the fight is over, then that off period leads fighters to think, *'Now what?'*"

Those closest to Paul always feared the answer.

Chapter 10: The Second Act

Paul fidgeted nervously with his cell phone. It was the summer of 2006 – more than three months since his liberation from Quehanna and nearly two years since his last professional bout – and Acri had yet to call with updates of an upcoming opponent. He was back in rehab again, a condition of his parole and a necessary step in his recovery, but each passing minute inched him closer to his thirty-first birthday. When the court denied his request to train with Steward in Detroit, Paul wondered whether his best days as a boxer had already ended.

The only thing he could do was wait, and it was excruciating. Paul occupied his free time by filling the vacant spaces on his body with more tattoos. Among his more evocative selections were two theater masks representing comedy and tragedy with the inscription, "Smile Now/Cry Later." The artwork was meant to be an indelible reminder that past indiscretions had cost him everything, but no tears or self-pity would fix his predicament. He could only commit to improving, and boxing needed to play a role in his revival.

Paul's spirits were raised when Acri gave him the green light to enter camp for a Thanksgiving Eve matchup against Shelbyville, Indiana, welterweight Jesus Franciso Zepeda. The fight particulars, however, encapsulated just how far he had fallen. It would take place at the Avalon Hotel in Erie for a measly five-figure sum. Paul's crimes had cost him his partnership with Iron City Brewery, and he could no longer afford to turn down any payday.

Moreover, Reid and Yankello were no longer under contract, and Paul would need to move ahead with a reconstructed team. Acri appointed Al Zuck as Paul's new trainer and Malcolm Garrett as his new cutman. Paul consented to the additions but lobbied for *some* familiarity – even if only for the night of the fight. "(Paul) begged me to come back and be in his corner for positivity, and it wasn't a big deal for me," Reid said. "It wasn't a binding thing. I never made a tremendous amount of money with Paul, but I loved him."

As much as it afflicted her, so did Nadine. She remained devoted, even in the wake of infidelity accusations that coerced Paul to call off their engagement. "Some of his friends would tell him I got married and pregnant again while he was at boot camp, but I wasn't doing anything except buying a French drain to make the house look nice and watching our baby," Nadine said. "I wanted to do these things for him because we had both been through a lot of things."

The struggle to stay together was taking its toll on them both. Nadine was prohibited from visiting Paul without the approval of a parole officer, so she commuted to Erie midweek and met with him in secrecy between his training sessions at Bizzarro's Gym before returning home on weekends to resume bartending. "We were a mix of Romeo and Juliet and Bonnie and Clyde," Nadine kidded. "We wanted to be together, but everything and everyone was not in favor."

The turmoil might have hampered Paul's regular training regimen, but Paul viewed Zepeda (16-3, nine knockouts) as a run-of-the-mill patsy with an active imagination. He was almost amused when Zepeda said in a press release, "What a great Thanksgiving this will be. I'm going to turn Spadafora's ring return into his ring retirement."

THE SECOND ACT

Paul cut Zepeda above his right eye midway through the first round and reopened it twice more, forcing referee Rick Steigerwald to call it in the fifth. "I didn't understand (fighting Zepeda)," Paul said. "Boxers like Diego Corrales go to jail, come out and fight on TV. *Paul* goes to jail and fights club-level guys."

The perceived slight made him more determined to make his bones at junior welterweight, although he would not show it in his subsequent bout.

Paul remained in Erie but paired up with a new trainer named Rick Diaz to ready himself for a March 9, 2007, matchup against Oisin "Gale Force" Fagan at the Soaring Eagle Casino in Mt. Pleasant, Michigan.

Fagan (17-3, 10 knockouts) of Dublin, Ireland, had won 11 consecutive fights and the Irish junior welterweight championship, though nine of his victories came against boxers with losing records. Paul expected to manhandle Fagan but fought tepidly in the early rounds. Fagan was more aggressive, and an upset almost seemed conceivable. In the later stages, Paul relied on his superior skill to barely squeeze out a majority split decision, and he was disgruntled with his effort.

Desperate to prove he had retained his competitive edge, Paul became obsessive about returning to camp immediately. After completing his post-prison rehab, he was driven to do things correctly. Nevertheless, he began to worry when his calendar remained open for several months following the Fagan win. After several more passed without any signal of another fight, paranoia set in, and Paul questioned if Acri had any interest in seeing him succeed.

The lull deepened his discontent with Nadine. Visitation restrictions aside, Paul became exasperated with their on–again, off–again drama and lost his temper in her presence regularly. In the same breath, he cared for her deeply and could not stay away.

Nadine filed a restraining order against him after a spat over her bartending job turned somewhat physical. Paul violated it, was arrested, and served 75 days in Pennsylvania's State Correctional Institution at Albion.

Then, when freed at the end of the summer, Paul and Nadine attempted to repair their relationship again.

It became a maddening cycle neither could escape.

Nadine grappled with her own doubts and insecurities. She traced the scar under her ribcage and considered the horrendous ordeal she had endured with Paul. The bullet from his gun had narrowly skimmed past her heart, but their explosive arguments continued to shatter it into pieces. She loved him but worried a permanent separation was unavoidable.

The final indignity was experienced the afternoon Geno bumped his head at a babysitter's house and was taken to Ohio Valley General Hospital. Doctors had already closed his incision with staples when Nadine arrived. She acted groggily – a side effect of the Seroquel she had taken the previous night to help her sleep – but snapped out of her daze when she peeked down the hallway. "Someone from Child Youth Services took my son and disappeared, and I flipped the fuck out," she said.

Nadine alleged she was told she was being charged with negligence because she had never signed documents authorizing another adult to admit Geno to the hospital in case of emergency. "I was 21 years old and didn't know that was even a thing," she said. "In the (Child Youth Services) report, it was stated our family friend had told

THE SECOND ACT

them she had Geno for weeks *on end*, but she really said it was only for that week-*END* when I was working."

The explanation garnered little sympathy from the police, who were knowledgeable about Nadine's background. "A cop told me, 'Maybe next time you'll press charges against Paul,'" she added. "They always hated him (after the shooting incident)."

Nadine left feeling crushed. She combatted her misery with heavy drinking and took extra Percocet to numb herself. She also used cocaine, which brought some unanticipated consequences. A drug test detected it in her urine on the day of the custody hearing, obliging the judge to terminate her parental rights.

The court placed Geno in foster care, and Child Youth Services mandated Paul and Nadine to separate as a condition of his return. Paul abided by the ruling and broke away from Nadine, realizing their illicit affair had caused enough damage. Acri made him change his phone number as an additional measure.

Nadine knew there were no guarantees that Paul and Geno would ever return. She felt the world had ripped them away, and she fell apart. "I was like an outsider in my own life," Nadine said. "I didn't know how to live like that, nor want to."

Instead of kicking the coke habit that cost her Geno, Nadine leaned on it more heavily and snorted enough lines to erode a hole through her septum.

She found rock bottom when she tried to score an ounce from an FBI informant for her and her friends. After she was arrested and charged with conspiracy to distribute, Nadine served three years under house arrest while awaiting trial, followed by 10 months in Philadelphia's Federal Detention Center, and then stayed in a halfway house for another three months. She completed two more years of probation, totaling what Nadine called "six years for partying."

The lengthy sentence empowered her to get clean and make a long-term plan to right her many wrongs.

"I was severely depressed and could have died doing coke with all of those (Percocet) pills," Nadine said. "Getting arrested helped me get my life together."

***

Paul put loyalty above all other qualities. It explained his lifelong affinity for dogs. He owned several over the years. They were jolly and affectionate creatures, and he could always count on them to have his back.

He exhibited that same level of allegiance to his closest friends. Paul would spare his last dollar if it would help them get through a jam and, like his beloved canines, would always have *their* backs.

Mike Kuster observed it the day he was sucker punched at a bar outside PNC Park. The blow, intended for Paul, rendered Kuster bloodied and baffled. A bouncer escorted him into a bathroom to apply first aid, but he heard about the aftermath. "Paul ran outside to fight him and screamed, 'You want to hurt my friend?'" Kuster said. "The guy stood on the other side of his car and didn't move. He didn't want no piece of him."

Kuster needed surgery to repair his eye and lost 20 teeth, but he gained a new admiration for Paul. "He was the only guy that ran out there for me."

Paul was equally willing to run through brick walls for Acri, even though it seemed like he was getting more opportunities to fight in the streets than in the ring. Paul was a fully-tatted former boxing champion of modest dimensions, making him a target for every wannabe tough guy in town. When inebriated enough, he was ready to take on any comers. When sober, he reminded himself that the barroom brawls led him nowhere and paid him nothing. He had long since traded in his Hummer to pay off debts and lost his Moon residence to the bank.

With his career rapidly approaching its expiration date, Paul blamed Acri for keeping him on the shelf.

The long-awaited announcement of an April 25, 2008, bout against Shad Howard provided little reassurance. Paul had torn a ligament in his knee that required surgery, but the recovery time would sideline him for months. Accordingly, he moved the procedure to a later date and trained through the pain. Paul had not boxed in over a year. He understood the necessity to emerge from his hibernation with a resounding victory, glumly comprehending he needed to remain relevant at any cost.

Howard (13-10, six knockouts) went the eight-round distance, but Paul landed more punches and was scarcely touched, making his unanimous decision at The Avalon look like a breeze. "I got the win. I'm back, and I'm ready to move on," he told the *Meadville Tribune*. "I'm definitely back. I feel great. This was a great chance for me to get back in the flow of things and the top 10."

To ensure such a surge, his management needed first to obtain him a top-10 opponent. Paul craved the cream of the junior welterweights but believed he was being force-fed its creampuffs in slow doses. Acri told reporters it was difficult rounding up fighters willing to scrap against a southpaw of Paul's pedigree, and Diaz emphasized the need to ease him back into action. Paul rebuked both explanations and vented to anyone who would listen. He was unbeaten in 41 bouts. He held the IBF lightweight belt and made eight successful title defenses. He had been a regular on ESPN and a headliner on HBO. He felt he deserved better.

After doctors repaired his knee, Paul moved his training to Malcolm Garrett's Gym in Indiana, Pennsylvania.

With the change in scenery came a long-awaited change in fortune.

Pernell Whitaker was Paul's idol for explicable reasons. Dubbed "Sweet Pete" by family, he became regularly known by his identifiable "Sweet *Pea*" moniker after a journalist misheard and misreported it while covering an early fight for a local newspaper.

As Whitaker rose through the ranks, no one would ever misinterpret his formidable skill. He was a smooth, counterpunching lefty with a psychic ring awareness. These traits, coupled with feline agility, framed Whitaker's reputation as a defensive genius and helped him win Olympic gold in 1984 and world championships in four different weight divisions.

Whitaker's rematch against Jose Luis Ramirez (winning him *The Ring* magazine and WBC championships) and victory over Juan Nazario (for the WBA belt) displayed his greatness. But it was his controversial 1993 majority draw against Julio César Chávez that Paul admired most. Whitaker defused Chávez with a relentless jab and eluded him from beginning to end, leading many pundits to believe the ringside judges helped Chávez (then 87-0 with 75 knockouts and deemed boxing's pound-for-pound best) pull off the heist of the century.

Paul was no exception. "(Whitaker) beat Chávez's ass!" he proclaimed. "I watched it over a thousand times.

THE SECOND ACT

Chávez is going down as one of the top fighters ever, and Pernell was beating him with one hand – his jab hand! He was that good. It was beautiful what he was doing."

Seeing Whitaker waiting for him at the end of a morning jog was an even better sight. Paul was starstruck and became tongue-tied as his hero spoke, but he hung on every word that spilled from his lips.

"What are you doing running five miles? Fighters should only be running two-and-a-half."

Once Paul told him he was without a sparring partner, Whitaker peered at Garrett and said, "If this motherfucker can't fight with anyone, then I'm outta here!'"

The scornful reaction was music to Paul's ears because its implication rang abundantly clear: Acri was gifting him a boxing brainiac with a relatable style that could propel him to uncharted heights.

The ensuing months would validate this assumption, and a close friendship developed. As their bond strengthened, Whitaker replenished Paul's optimism that he could capture another world championship in his new weight division. "It was unbelievable training with (Whitaker)," Paul said. "I stole so much knowledge from him. I couldn't understand how Pernell talked because he had a lot more fights than me – more than 300 (amateur). He fought everyone. So what I did was I watched all of his fights, and then, whenever he would tell me something, I would watch them (again), and it just clicked. He was a superstar."

He was also the reason Paul looked recharged during his June 19, 2009, return to the I.C. Light Amphitheater to face Argentina's Ivan Orlando Bustos (25-12-3, eight knockouts). With a Hall of Fame inductee guiding his every move, Paul threw punches with a vengeance. Bustos was overwhelmed by the bombardment, spurring his trainer to stop the fight before the end of the sixth.

Paul barely had time to celebrate his technical knockout before being rushed into another camp to train for a September 30 faceoff with Gary, Indiana's Jermaine "Too Sweet" White (17-3, 10 knockouts). The bout would be held under the Heinz Field VIP Tent. It was a far cry from the cavernous confines of the Petersen Events Center and The Harv but fittingly adjacent to the gridiron of an NFL squad that had just won its sixth Super Bowl on the strength of allowing the fewest yards and points per game.

On fight night, Paul did his best impersonation of the vaunted Steelers defense by limiting White from mounting any offense. He also blitzed him with an unremitting jab and a sequence of combos through the middle and later rounds, all of which helped him lock up a unanimous decision.

Whitaker seemed satisfied but weighed the level of competition and wanted more. Paul dished out punches with more accuracy and authority under his watch, but Whitaker grasped gains in the gym meant nothing if his fighter prepared for nonentities. "We get a champion, we'll show them how good you look," he told Paul in front of reporters.

Their next opponent fit Whitaker's description – at least technically. Italy's Ivan Fiorletta (24-5-2, eight knockouts) had acquired the vacant IBF Intercontinental Super Featherweight Title and some lesser-regarded belts, but he was unranked and largely unknown in the states. The March 13, 2010 bout, scheduled more than six months after Paul's latest win, yielded minimal benefit. "I was getting mad at Mike (Acri) and Al (McCauley) because I

THE SECOND ACT

wasn't fighting anyone," Paul said. "I thought when Pernell came in, that would all change."

Whitaker impatiently assumed nothing ever would. He shuffled behind Paul into the War Memorial Auditorium in Fort Lauderdale, Florida, like a desk jockey preparing for a dreary day at the office. He watched Paul land combinations to Fiorletta's head in the second, then alternate with attacks to the head and body in the middle rounds. After Fiorletta's left eye began swelling, Referee Frank Gentile stopped the fight early in the eighth.

The technical knockout victory extended Paul's record to 44-0-1, but its insignificance brought forth a demoralizing loss when Whitaker tendered his resignation.

"Pernell told Mike, 'If Paul ain't fighting someone real, I'm not gonna be here,'" Paul said. "He was finished."

Paul reacted to the departure like it was a death in the family. Whitaker was an icon – one the greatest the boxing world had ever witnessed – and he had also become one of Paul's closest confidants. In his absence, Paul became consumed by a familiar emptiness, and his natural inclination was to self-medicate with whatever frothy elixir was on tap at the pub.

Acri continued to guarantee negotiations for bigger fights were underway, but he experienced setbacks. Paul was being shopped for a bout against WBC lightweight champion Edwin Valero before Valero hanged himself inside a jail cell a day after being arrested for murdering his wife. Proposed matchups against Mexican lightweight Erik Morales and Argentina's Diego Jesus Ponce also fell through.

Without Whitaker, the end only appeared closer. Paul would soon turn 35. He shuddered to contemplate life after boxing because he had never attempted to learn anything else. Since Harry had first taken him to a gym, it was the only thing he wanted to do.

Paul was temporarily appeased when a November 20 bout was scheduled against Alain Hernandez (18-9, 10 knockouts). It would be hosted at the Mohegan Sun Casino in Uncasville, Connecticut, the site of the first war in the epic Micky Ward–Arturo Gatti trilogy. The venue's size and the slightly larger paycheck he was offered insinuated progress. Winning became a foregone conclusion when he heard Reid would fly out to lend his support.

And given the uncertainty that he would ever again compete at a high level, Paul needed his performance to be explosive.

That night, he channeled eight months of aggravation into the punches he detonated on Hernandez's head and torso. The combos caused enough damage each round to keep his hapless rival from returning for the sixth. "(Hernandez) wasn't the same caliber as I was," Paul said.

At 45-0-1 with 19 knockouts, few were. Paul had done everything to market himself as a welterweight contender and attributed any lapse in his sobriety to prolonged inactivity. "I'm just waiting on the promotor," he said. "Whenever they give me the date, whenever the guy comes forward, I'll be there! All you got to do is tell me when, and I'll be there."

Following four-and-a-half years of a fruitless second act, Paul deliberated if Acri could ever again deliver him anyone of value. The juice had never been worth the squeeze, and he despondently resigned himself to the

THE SECOND ACT

ludicrous realization that he was becoming a washed-up has-been who had never been defeated.

He had all but given up totally before being apprised of a secret weapon that had unknowingly been concealed in his back pocket – one that packed the potency to change his resentment overnight.

Paul never needed to watch the footage of his sparring session with Floyd Mayweather Jr. More than a decade later, he could visualize every nuance with high-definition clarity. But he became intrigued when told the recording had been leaked online and had generated impassioned debate among fight fanatics who clamored to see the two champions settle the score in a real bout.

When Acri informed Paul in January of 2011 that Don King and Mayweather's management brass had approached him about a possible deal, Paul's intrigue morphed into jaw-dropping bewilderment.

The idea was born from a longer-running proposal to pit Mayweather, an unbeaten world champion in five weight classes, against Manny Pacquiao, another world champion in eight weight classes, in what both sides foresaw to be the highest-grossing boxing event in history.

Since Pacquiao was also a lefty, Paul presented a tempting tune-up option. "Paul is interested in the fight," Acri told BoxingScene.com. "He's wanted this fight for a very long time. Paul is ready to finish what he started 10 years ago. We'll see what happens."

Mayweather (41-0, 25 knockouts) had emerged as one of the biggest draws in all sports. After splitting with Top Rank and starting his self-named Mayweather Promotions firm in 2007, he also surfaced as one of the wealthiest, so much so that he had long since ditched his "Pretty Boy" label in favor of "Money."

A 10 percent cut from a Mayweather purse would net Paul millions. "(Floyd Jr.) would love to do that with Spadafora," verified Mayweather's father, Floyd Sr., during an interview with OnTheRopesBoxingRadio.com. "As a matter of fact, Spadafora is trying to get the money right now. That's what he needs. If he needs the money, he can get it. If he needs a whupping, he can get it, and a whupping he's going to get because if he takes the fight, that's what's going to happen."

The disparaging commentary made Paul ecstatic. It meant he was not only back in the game but in an *immense* way. He returned to the gym and trained as if his life depended on it because, in many ways, he sensed it did.

More importantly, he also analyzed videos of Mayweather's wins. The renowned shoulder roll that made him unhittable against right-handers was less effective against esteemed lefties like DeMarcus Corley and Zab Judah. Both found holes and connected with rare, clean shots, even though neither had a response for Mayweather's lead right and left hook. Paul was confident his angling and slippery movement set up a defensive counterpunch Mayweather had never encountered in a sanctioned fight.

Their theoretical bout would be airtight, but Paul believed he had the perfect style to pull off the upset.

A victory, he envisaged, would be his magnum opus, an unparalleled moment that would distinguish him as one of the greatest defensive technicians who ever lived.

***

In the end, Mayweather killed Paul's dream without throwing a single punch.

THE SECOND ACT

"My fans have been waiting long enough," he Tweeted. "Floyd Mayweather vs. Victor Ortiz. Sept-17 2011 for the WBC World Championship."

Paul imploded. "All year long, I was told I'm fighting Mayweather," he said. "I had went (almost) a year without fighting anyone. I didn't even have enough money to buy a soda. I thought, 'No Mayweather fight, I'm done.'"

And by *done*, Paul meant he was ready to *die*. He hit the streets, scored his first ounce of heroin, snorted it all in an alley, and waited to take his final breath on a friend's bed.

Paul was found unresponsive and rushed by ambulance to Allegheny General Hospital. Doctors revived him and he was released, but the overdose did not change his emotional state. He hid in the shadows of abandoned buildings that lacked heat, running water, and electricity for weeks. He used coke. When that ran out, he smoked crack.

During weaker moments, he clutched an AK-47 against his lap and cried himself to sleep as he entertained sinister scenarios. "I was ready to rob and kill a drug dealer," Paul said. "I had it justified in my mind."

He suppressed that whim but no longer had qualms about voicing his irritation with Acri. "(Paul) wanted me to stay with him but wanted to get rid of Mike, and I wasn't going to leave Mike," McCauley said. "(Acri) was the one who put Paul into position to get another title."

At that point, none of it mattered. Many months behind on child support payments, Paul continued using drugs and was arrested twice that fall for drunk driving. Gaunt, disheveled, and devoid of all hope, he figured it was only a matter of time before a cemetery plot beckoned his name.

Fortunately for Paul, he was blessed to have friends in high places who wanted to see him reclaim control of a life and legacy they believed was worth saving.

Marco Machi, owner and lead trainer of The Exercise Warehouse in Bloomfield, took pity and persuaded Paul to work at his gym. In exchange, Machi permitted him to stay in an empty apartment on the facility's second floor. The move was not a final remedy but a crucial, preliminary step that forced Paul to slow down. It also facilitated visits with his son, who was still under the primary care of a foster family. "Geno went to Immaculate Conception (School), and when it would let out, I would pick him up and take him to my crib," he said.

Paul's demeanor improved further that winter when he was approached by Ray Ventrone, a pal affiliated with the local chapter of the Pittsburgh Boilermaker's Union, and presented with a paid sponsorship to attend Transitions Recovery Program. The posh drug and alcohol treatment center in North Miami Beach, Florida, served an upscale clientele that included Hollywood celebs and professional athletes.

The offer was too enticing to snub. "(Ventrone) told me, 'I feel sorry for you. You were *The Pittsburgh Kid*, and you look bad. You need to get help,'" Paul said. "It was freezing outside. What else was I going to do."

Paul flew to "The Sunshine State" and embarked on a seven-month cleanse that shook him to his core. As a boxer, he intrinsically kept his gloves elevated to protect himself. But at Transitions, he let down his guard and exposed his vulnerability. He unloaded anecdotes about his relationship with his dad, his day-to-day survival with

THE SECOND ACT

a sex offender, the losses of Pecora and his Pap, his many arrests, the inexcusable morning he nearly killed Nadine, and his compulsive self-destruction. He left no stone unturned. "I had to sit in front of people and tell my life story," Paul said. "I cried because it hurt so bad. I had to do some real soul-searching."

Searching for a new promoter became an additional priority during his visit. But to accomplish that feat, he would first need to leave the one who had helped make him a world champion.

In the winter of 2012, Paul severed ties with Acri and McCauley (based on McCauley's insistence that they came as a package). Paul loved them both and hated thinking about ending an alliance that spanned more than 15 years, but he saw it as his only option. "My mind was made up when I talked it over with my counselors," Paul said. "I wasn't going back to using heroin."

Going back to the gym seemed more logical. Drumming a speed bag usually led him to better things. The staff at Transitions accommodated Paul by building him a personal training facility on its grounds.

And sure enough, the puzzle pieces for a *second* comeback organically fell into place.

It started when New Jersey-based manager Pat Lynch caught wind of Paul's whereabouts. Lynch had steered the storied careers of world champions Al Cole, Ray Mercer, Charles Murray, and Gatti. In Paul, he saw an undefeated fighter with something left in the tank, so he sent Robert Ortense, a friend and fellow boxing buff who spent his winters in Florida, to meet Paul and investigate his availability.

Lynch's interest waned upon hearing Paul was bound to McCauley. Ortense, oppositely, was enamored with

Paul's potential to make another title run. Sensing an opportunity to be part of something huge, he used Lynch's connections to pair Paul with renowned trainer Mikey Rod and former IBF light welterweight and WBC welterweight champion James "Buddy" McGirt.

Within days, they would begin training in Fort Lauderdale. Within months, Ortense would unofficially assume the role as Paul's new manager and score him a meeting with Wilfredo Negron (26-16,-1, 19 knockouts) on a Tampa card with Fight Night Productions.

When Acri and McCauley expectedly objected and pulled the bout, Ortense brought Joe Horn into the fray.

Horn was an ex-cop turned attorney. He was also Ortense's nephew-in-law through marriage and a boxing fan who was well-versed with Paul's legal dossier. "Paul had a whole host of issues... a suspended license and open criminal cases," Horn said. "I was brought on to be the guy with the mop and the bucket to clean up the legal aspect of all of this."

Paul's contractual restraints took precedence. After wrangling through preliminary resistance from the Pennsylvania State Athletic Commission, Horn blocked McCauley that June from extending his agreement with Paul past its expiration date. Then, to further protect him, he and Ortense settled his tab. "(Paul) owed a lot in child support, and that gives the Commonwealth the authority to suspend a boxing license," Horn said. "Bobby and I got him all caught up (with his payments), so there was nothing that would come back and bite us."

Before divorcing Paul from Acri, Horn shopped around for a new promotional outfit, a process expedited by Paul's eagerness to rehire Tom Yankello as his trainer.

THE SECOND ACT

Since prepping Paul for his last title defense, Yankello had made a sizeable splash in the boxing scene. In addition to guiding Monty Meza-Clay to an International Boxing Association (IBA) super featherweight championship, Yankello had come extremely close to coaching IBF heavyweight Calvin Brock and WBO cruiserweight Brian Minto to world titles. He was also in the process of training eight-time world champion Roy Jones Jr.

During a telecast, ESPN Boxing Analyst Joe Tessitore even sang Yankello's praises. "If I were managing a fighter and needed a trainer who could take us all the way, Tom Yankello would be on my shortlist," he declared. "What he does with his talent is very impressive. His passion and enthusiasm for the sport, and his commitment to his fighters, is as good as anybody's."

Paul had always been conscious of these virtues but was most interested in linking up with someone who understood him above all others. He reached out to Yankello during his stay at Transitions, and those old feelings were reciprocated. "Without boxing, I was going to die or be in jail, and you couldn't let me alone with my boys down in (McKees) Rocks because I was always in trouble," Paul said. "As a trainer, Tommy was like I was – obsessed with the game. And I knew if there was anyone I was gonna train with, it would be a guy that would let me box the way I knew how to box and would also be on me like flies on shit. That's all I needed."

Under Yankello's recommendation, Paul signed with TNT Promotions, a burgeoning enterprise led by Troy and Tammy Ridgley, Yankello's brother Mark, and advised by Jones Jr. "Paul was once at the top, and he could get back to the top with the right people around him," Jones Jr. told *Sports Illustrated*. "Not many people would want to take a chance on him, but we're willing to take that gamble and see what happens."

Paul was anxious to prove TNT had played their cards correctly. He left Transitions that July and returned to Pennsylvania to train with Yankello for his first assignment – an August 18, 2012, welterweight matchup against Negron, the boxer he was initially booked to meet.

Acri sued Paul for violating their promotional contract, but Horn and TNT attorney Steve Toprani delayed litigation by taking the fight outside Pennsylvania after influencing West Virginia's Mountaineer Racetrack and Casino lawyers to stage it at The Harv.

Paul was a month shy of turning 37 and would revisit the ring following his second-longest layoff.

Yet mentally, physically, and spiritually, he felt every bit of a man reborn.

***

Humberto "Bam Baby" Toledo (41-8-2, 25 knockouts) replaced Negron a week before the bout. The Ecuadorian held the WBC Latino Super Featherweight and Fecarbox lightweight titles. He was a step up in status.

To Paul, he was another journeyman who would get trounced.

But even Tom Yankello was astounded at how assertively Paul would do it that evening. He evaded punches, landed his jab at will, and appeared to enjoy himself. This was especially evident in the second round when Paul bludgeoned Toledo with a right that sent his mouthpiece sailing into the third row. "Paul was rejuvenated," Tom Yankello said. "He was on his game like he had never left. I just believed he could win a world title again."

The TNT team would settle for a vigorous eight-round unanimous decision before an energetic audience that included Crystal Connor, Nadine, and a new girl Paul had been dating during his stint at Transitions. "I felt really good," Paul said. "(Toledo) got a good beating. I had been clean for a really long time and could've fought anyone."

McCauley continued pursuing his own fight by filing a lawsuit to save their old contract, but Horn shoved back and swayed McCauley and Acri into dropping their claims that fall. Though contentious and unpleasant, the victory was more significant to Paul than the one he earned against Toledo. It enabled him to concentrate on boxing and nothing more.

The lion's share of Paul's take from the Toledo gate – estimated to be in the tens of thousands – covered unpaid billing statements and debts owed to previous landlords. The rest financed Paul's food and rent at a two-story brick house owned by Tom Yankello across the street from his gym. The living and training arrangement ensured stability, a non-negotiable prerequisite for Paul's return to prominence.

And with TNT, he was well on his way. Paul had climbed to number 11 among WBA junior welterweights before battling Solomon Egberime on December 1 at The Harv.

Egberime (22-3-1, 11 knockouts) was an ex-Olympian from Nigeria and erstwhile Australian and Oriental super lightweight champion making his American debut. He was also fourteenth in the WBO, making him Paul's highest-ranked rival since Dorin.

Nonetheless, Paul likened himself to a man who had risen from the dead. He stepped into the ring wearing a black robe with "A Phoenix Rising" imprinted across its back. The words symbolized his road to redemption and revealed he was a changed person. He wore his hair twisted into cornrows for the occasion and even looked different.

His counterpunching prowess was still recognizable, though Egberime would make him earn every inch.

Paul measured Egberime with lukewarm jabs through the first two rounds. Egberime threw a hard right to Paul's chin in the third, but Paul caught him with a left and several combos in the fourth. Egerberime answered aggressively in the fifth and the sixth and returned to his corner each time sucking wind. He was gutsy, but Paul was in better condition and defensively superior.

Egberime wounded Paul's right eye with a headbutt in the ninth, but Paul avenged it with a clean two-punch combo to Egberime's face in the tenth.

Both boxers stared each other down after the final bell, chest-to-chest, before peeling away to await the judges' scores. Paul led the punch count and controlled most of the rounds, so he was unmoved when it was announced that he had taken another unanimous decision. "Good fighter," Paul said of Egberime. "Angles, positioning... I made it where the only person he'd be able to hurt was himself, and it was a boring-ass Paul Spadafora fight."

It was also a Spadafora *victory* that would extend his record to 47-0-1 and place him at number eight in the IBF.

TNT quickly entered negotiations in January of 2013 to get Paul in the ring against a rising star named Vernon Paris, whose only loss came by a ninth-round technical knockout to Judah. A strong performance over Paris could

THE SECOND ACT

plant Paul into discussions as a worthy challenger for WBC lightweight champion Adrian Broner or WBA welterweight champion Paulie Malignaggi.

While awaiting word, Paul joined Horn at his summer home in Bergen, New Jersey. He ran the boardwalk and trained with strength-and-conditioning coach Dave Paladino. Under the terms of his TNT contract, Paul also collaborated with Horn to reform his image through speaking engagements warning children about making wise choices in the presence of drugs and alcohol.

Upon discovering talks to fight Paris had disintegrated, Paul returned to Garnic's wooded compound that March to prepare for Paris's replacement – a scrappy gatekeeper named Rob Frankel.

At 32-12-1 with six knockouts, a Frankel fight initially seemed like a lateral move. He was Adrian Broner's sparring partner, and Paul would have obviously preferred signing to box Broner. But the April 6 bout would mark Paul's third in eight months, and the victor would at least attain the vacant NABF super lightweight belt. "I always thought to compete for a NABF title, you have to be a good fighter," Paul said. "(Frankel) didn't seem like someone who should be fighting for this."

Paul reinforced this assertion against Frankel early and often. After getting popped with a jab to the nose in the first round, Paul opened a cut below Frankel's right eye with a searing left in the second.

Following a conservatively-paced third, Paul unlocked his arsenal by spreading jabs, hooks, and uppercuts to Frankel's head and body. He opened a considerable gash above Frankel's left eye in the sixth. The blood distorted Frankel's vision, enabling Paul to wail away with consistent rights.

By the end of round 10, Frankel's mug resembled a slaughterhouse floor, and Paul would obtain a messy unanimous decision. "Frankel was a rugged kid who could hurt ya, but Paul walked through him," Horn said. "The personal trainer (Paladino) worked Paul's legs and stamina and strength in a way that Paul had never done before, and it brought out a whole different element."

With his new title in hand and circulating mention that Paul was only a victory shy of tying Rocky Marciano's 49-0 undefeated streak, TNT anticipated it finally had its promotional elements lined up to lure an eminent opponent. But securing boxers of any standing proved onerous. Paul was still seen as a skilled southpaw who could make any fighter look inept. He also was no longer considered a major draw, and TNT could not offer a purse large enough to make it worthwhile.

Mark Yankello nearly signed Paul to a bout with Puerto Rican prospect Thomas Dulorme before negotiations faltered that summer when the original proposal – a featured headliner on HBO's *Boxing After Dark* – was relegated to airtime on HBO Latino, an offshoot subscription service with limited U.S. availability. "When Paul upsets the apple cart versus a guy like Dulorme in his continuance of one of the great comebacks in recent U.S. history, shouldn't it be seen by all fans in this country?" Mark Yankello asked the *Pittsburgh City Paper*, adding that the altered contract would have netted Paul "less money than he can make putting on a sparring exhibition."

With retirement looming, Paul sought paydays that could set him up in perpetuity. Following numerous conversations with Golden Boy matchmaker Roberto Diaz, Mark Yankello was finally presented with a premier

THE SECOND ACT

opportunity. "(Diaz) had this Venezuelan kid named Johan Perez who was a (former) WBA champion, but said they didn't have a market for him in the U.S.," he explained. "So Diaz told me if you want to put on an event and pay for it, he would take Spadafora on (with Golden Boy). The contract was fully executed, but the mechanism for a four-fight term was predicated upon a Spadafora victory over Perez."

Paul needed no further explanation and agreed to challenge Perez (17-1-1, 12 knockouts) for the interim WBA light welterweight belt in a deal Mark Yankello said included "nice, minimum economic terms that could put Paul on *Showtime Boxing*" and would expose him to six-figure earnings.

Tom Yankello always liked Paul's chances but realized there would be no cakewalk to victory. After losing the WBA belt to Pablo Caser Cano in 2012 following an accidental headbutt that severely cut Cano above his right eye, Perez rebounded to score a unanimous decision over Yoshihiro Kamegai (22-0, 18 knockouts) and a majority decision over former IBF super featherweight champion Steve Forbes. He was the number-three ranked WBA contender and, at 5-foot-11, stood two inches taller than anyone Paul had encountered. His gangly reach enabled him to score easily from the outside, and he threw hooks with surprising power.

The matchup would be cumbersome, and Paul came into training camp for their November 30 battle at The Harv with explicit instructions. "Dorin was a short guy who wanted to fight Paul from the inside," Tom Yankello said. "Paul also needed to be the better guy on the inside for this fight, and I knew (Paul) had a better inside-fighting game than Perez. Paul had to take the fight *to him*."

Adjustments were made, and a new strategy was honed before Tom Yankello claimed Paul made a demand that became a hindrance. "Horn brings in McGirt the last two weeks, and (McGirt) is pushing Paul to box as a pure boxer," he said. "Buddy is a great trainer, and he has a lot of knowledge, but he didn't know Paul like I did, and he thought Paul needed to *remain* a pure boxer who fought from the outside. When you have two different trainers spitting two different things, all it will do is confuse a fighter."

Paul could only work toward striking a balance the evening of the bout. Two years earlier, he was a cautionary tale living on borrowed time. But now he entered The Harv with the steely glare of a man attempting to complete the unfathomable.

The capacity crowd cheered in adoration as Paul strutted to the ring wearing black-and-gold gladiator garb. He felt ready to overtake Perez on sheer adrenaline alone.

Perez was also focused, but the event's immensity did not appear to hit him as intensely. "I was walking in the casino earlier and saw Perez in the lobby licking an ice cream cone, just relaxing," Horn said. "I told Bobby (Ortense) he's either ignorant of what's about to happen, or he's very comfortable and is going to give Paul a very hard time tonight."

Horn's initial hunch seemed more likely in the first round. Paul boxed comfortably, scored with a few lefts, and efficiently avoided Perez's offense.

Perez nailed Paul with a hard right to start the second and followed up with a solid right-left combo to Paul's head. Paul dipped under some of Perez's swings and connected with a few counterpunches but failed to land as many shots.

THE SECOND ACT

Paul's defensive wizardry took over in the third. He absorbed a right hook but largely avoided Perez's salvo by shifting, blocking, and dipping away. In some instances, he made Perez miss widely.

But Perez hit his stride in the fourth with consecutive blows that sliced a gaping cut above Paul's left eye and bruised another spot below his right. He was finding his range and making contact with regularity, and Paul struggled to react.

Tom Yankello commanded Paul to move in closer and throw his fists. "You've gotta keep coming!" he squawked. "Quit bobbing and weaving on this guy! (Perez) ain't got nothing!"

Paul tried to dictate the pace in the fifth but lunged with his punches and fought from a distance. Perez creamed Paul with a hard right. Paul slowly discovered he could not extend his arm without wincing. "(Paul) started having (left) elbow trouble after years of hyperextending and jamming it, and he never took care of it," Tom Yankello said. "It was an accumulation over time, and then he jammed it again."

With the pain intensifying, Paul pressed on intrepidly and opened a cut below Perez's right eye in the sixth round. But Perez knocked Paul off kilter by readjusting his stance and reapplying pressure from both inside and outside. He was also targeting the laceration above Paul's eye with hard lefts, and the wound hemorrhaged well into the seventh despite cutman Garnic's diligent efforts to keep it covered.

Perez continued stretching his lead in the eighth by widening the cut above Paul's eye. Paul showed moxie in the ninth and tenth rounds but was slightly outpointed because of Perez's nonstop jabs and unrelenting right cross.

His elbow throbbed, and his offense stalled. Still, Paul remained calm, knowing he always saved his best for last. "I thought to myself, *I'm going to end up killing this young motherfucker in the later rounds,*" he said.

True to form, Paul connected with body shots and squirmed away from Perez's punches to take the eleventh. "Buzzy told me, 'If you win the twelfth, you win the fight,'" Paul said. "I thought I could slide it in."

And he usually could. But Paul's outlook turned dire when Perez landed several lefts and rights to ensure an even more debatable outcome.

The bout stipulations permitted TNT to appoint two of the three mandated judges, and Mark Yankello had hand-picked West Virginia's Rex Agin and James Tia. As Gianna, Giovanna, and Geno meandered through the post-fight horde with pointer fingers hoisted proudly in support of their dad, Paul prayed his hometown advantage would pull him through.

Seconds later, his breathing stiffened as he watched his adversary jump onto the ring post in jubilation when it was announced that Agin had scored the bout 117-111 and Tia 115-113, and the third visiting judge, Glen Feldman of Connecticut, ruled it a draw, giving Perez the split majority decision.

Paul sullenly trekked back to his dressing room. "What I did poorly was not throw enough punches," he said matter-of-factly. "I should have been on him more. I should have been busier. I should have let my hands go."

Tom Yankello spun Paul's first defeat as an advantage in front of TV cameras a few feet away. "A lot of times in the past, people avoided him because, basically, there was

THE SECOND ACT

nothing to win and everything to lose. Now, maybe these guys will think a little less of him, and he will get even more opportunities because they'll think they could beat him."

Paul was too shaken to think that far ahead. He had failed his objective and, without the WBA belt, became convinced there was nothing else.

"I started drinking and drinking and drinking, and that led to more drinking, and the drinking led back to drugs, and it just never stopped," he said. "After that title fight, there was no more *Paul the boxer*. There was only *Paul the demon*."

Chapter 11: A Fallen Star

Tom Yankello continued presenting Paul's future through a positive lens in the days leading up to his July 11, 2014, main event bout against Hector Velazquez as part of TNT's "Rumble on the River 4."

"I think (Paul) is better than he was last fight," he told the *Beaver County Times*. "I feel like he is happier. He got the monkey off his back. (The unbeaten streak) was always on your mind. Sometimes, it's a blessing in disguise that he was able to persevere through adversity for the first time. That's uncharted waters for him, but it's made him a better fighter. He is a stronger fighter now, no doubt. How many guys have retired undefeated? Every great fighter has come back from a loss or come back from some kind of adversity to be a better and stronger fighter. Our goal is the same: Be world champion again. Nothing has changed."

In the eight months since falling to Perez, Paul knew nothing could be more misleading. He tried to bounce back that winter when Roberto Diaz told *The Ring* that Golden Boy was still interested in signing him to a contract. Diaz even disclosed pie-in-the-sky plans to put him on a Fox Sports 1 card by March.

Paul waited patiently for further developments as the date came and passed and was rewarded with silence.

Soon after, Paul's unranked sparring partner, "Lightning" Rod Salka (19-3, three knockouts), was selected to challenge WBA and WBC light welterweight champion Danny Garcia. Paul was happy for his friend but sorely aware the opportunity would likely have been offered to him had he taken care of business. "After Perez,

A FALLEN STAR

Paul spiraled into a depression," Horn said. "I'm sure there was drinking to reconcile that defeat."

Only Paul comprehended the true extent. "I was blasted the entire (Velazquez) camp," he said. "There was alcohol, pot, and cocaine. I wasn't sleeping."

As a result, he *was sleeping* hard on a competent adversary.

Velazquez (56-21-3, 28 knockouts) of Tijuana, Mexico, had won the IBA Continental Americas featherweight title in 2000 before losing world championship bouts to Manny Pacquiao (by sixth-round technical knockout for the WBC International super featherweight belt in 2005) and Edwin Valero (by sixth-round referee stoppage for the WBC lightweight belt in 2009). He was accomplished and, at 39 years old, very durable.

Paul did not intend to take Velazquez lightly, but he was also approaching 39 and feeling jaded.

As he made his way down the aisle at Pittsburgh's Rivers Casino sporting a shaved head and black trunks lined in the red, white, and green colors of the flag of Italy, Paul almost resembled the indestructible livewire who conquered Cardona 15 years earlier. But internally, he was an aging warrior who dreaded becoming a dinosaur in a sport that might soon forget him.

In the presence of 1,200 fans, that same warrior fell into a groove that night and showed hints of the "Spaddy" from yesteryear. Paul took flight in the second round by making Velazquez whiff on several punches, then jolted the crowd to attention when he thumped Velazquez with a left that drew blood above his right eye in the third. Velazquez gestured for him to bring more, and Paul complied by landing two whizzing rights.

Paul socked Velazquez in the abdomen with another right in the fourth, and then both boxers gave spectators their money's worth by exchanging a volley of blows before returning to their corners.

Tensions simmered in the sixth after Paul skirted a right, twirled Velazquez, and thrust two punches into his back.

It was a dirty maneuver, but Velazquez seemed most troubled about his inability to hurt Paul.

Velazquez advanced belligerently in the seventh and eighth but was repelled by Paul's jab and repeated clinching each time he approached too closely. Velazquez continued swinging in frustration after the final bell and demanded a rematch when learning Paul won handily by all three scorecards.

Paul (49-1-1, 19 knockouts) finished his assignment and had no desire to see Velazquez again despite getting no other offers. Mark Yankello worked around the clock for weeks to land Paul a fight against Broner. When those talks unraveled, Paul felt TNT had expended every option.

He grimaced that August as he watched Garcia stop Salka with a scorching left in the second round of their fight at the Barclays Center in Brooklyn, New York. He also marveled at the arena's dimensions and reminisced about headlining events of equal enormity. He half-heartedly wondered if he had anything left to give and was ready to concede the death of his career just days before a famous boxing *dad* granted it a stay of execution.

Paul could not believe his ears when Kenny Porter invited him to train in Las Vegas with him and his son, IBF welterweight champion Shawn Porter. The Porter family was well-respected, very connected, and regularly worked with a talented rotation of fighters. Geno, furthermore, had recently relocated to Vegas with Nadine, where she had begun working as a bartender and cocktail waitress.

Everything lined up almost too perfectly, and Paul took it as a sign.

Heeding the advice of friends, Paul extricated himself from TNT, Ortense, and Horn by filing bankruptcy. Horn contested it initially but soon after dropped his case. "I wasn't going to fight hard to keep him where he didn't want to be like others did in the past," he said. "Mark (Yankello) did a good job of not bailing on him and trying to make the best of the (Perez) loss, but Paul seemed like he wanted a clean slate."

And he wanted it without further delay.

Paul booked a one-way flight and hit the ground running. He sparred against Shawn Porter at the H.I.T. Factory Boxing Gym. He went multiple rounds with Devin Haney, an amateur phenom who would later win four world titles at lightweight. Once insiders bandied Zab Judah as a prospective matchup, Paul even allowed himself to get excited again.

But then, in early 2015, reality slapped Paul in the face when he was matched against unknown welterweight Jake Giuriceo as a late undercard addition on the February 20 "Pride of Pittsburgh III" show at the Consol Energy Center. Paul agreed to the bout initially but withdrew later, citing illness. "Who the fuck was I even training for," he said. "There were no (creditable) fights. It was all just talk."

Adding to his angst was the slow erosion of his quick-twitch reflexes and his once impermeable defense, leading him to sustain more shots to the head and body during his stay with the Porters than he had in the 25 previous years combined.

He was kidding himself. "I tried out there," Paul conceded, "but I just didn't have it anymore."

And with no signal that Golden Boy would ever follow through with its original intention to affix his name to its stable, Paul walked off into the sunset, once and for all, by way of the nearest liquor store.

He had no definitive plans moving forward, and it terrified him.

***

After returning to Pennsylvania, Paul used his IBF pension to purchase a simple two-bedroom house in Green Tree and found work stocking delivery trucks for United Parcel Service (UPS). He spent his evenings in local boxing gyms. Paul coached Geno through his first amateur bouts before he left for Nevada and liked sharing his knowledge with anyone who would listen.

But around friends, he groused over lost opportunities, especially during the summer of 2015 when the movie *Southpaw* reached theaters. Paul contends representatives of the Weinstein Brothers flew him to New York City during his stay at Transitions to educate themselves about his life before writing a screenplay inspired by his own. Different, nonetheless, was an ending featuring fictitious light heavyweight Billy Hope (played by Jake Gyllenhaal) finding redemption by recapturing a world title.

Paul never received compensation for his assistance with the project but took some consolation knowing he had at least procured his place among Pittsburgh's all-time fighting greats. He clung to this distinction with pride, knowing it could never be taken from him. He paid a

A FALLEN STAR

graffiti artist to paint a multihued image of himself recoiling from a punch along the back wall of his family room, then had him cover the other three with visuals of Billy Conn, Fritzie Zivic, Harry Greb, Sammy Angott, and Charley Burley. He enriched the décor by installing heavy and speed bags beside his couch. The modifications brought Paul comfort.

None of it helped him accept that his glory days were no more.

Neighbors would usually see Charlie with Paul. He was his closest companion and could usually perk him up. Paul and Charlie lived intermittently as roommates and shared good times and many adventures, just as they did throughout childhood.

As adults, they also shared incapacitating addictions. For Charlie, it was crack cocaine, a habit he developed at 16. Paul used the drug sparingly during his lowest moments, but Paul said Charlie would have smoked the pipe every day had he been able to afford it.

Charlie was unemployed but got by with the disability checks he received because of his Schizophrenia disorder. His medication made him spacey, and adding narcotics into his system only increased the frequency of his erratic behavior. Mark Haak recollected a time he spotted Charlie jogging in Lawrenceville, a riverfront neighborhood on the other side of the city. "I'm driving along, stop the car and say, 'Charlie, what are you doing,'" Haak described. "He said, 'I woke up and decided to run this morning.' (Charlie) told me he started in McKees Rocks, and that meant he had to cross a couple of bridges. It's after two in the afternoon, and he's just running down the street in a totally different town."

By his own admission, Paul's alcoholism was making him similarly unstable. After discovering in April 2016 that a girlfriend he was seeing was pregnant with his child, Paul went to the Redstone Tavern in Crafton to celebrate. He lost track of the number of drinks he ingested that afternoon but remembered getting ornery when he was cut off, prompting him to steal several swigs from an unattended beer. It instigated a heated argument when a 63-year-old female patron returned to retrieve her beverage a minute later. The bartender would later tell KDKA-TV News that Paul took the woman's hat, threw it, and "shook her in a headlock a little bit."

Paul alleged the woman spat on him before the altercation spilled into the parking lot, where video surveillance caught him throwing her to the pavement and fleeing the scene with Charlie.

Police apprehended Paul later that day at a Sheetz convenience store in Kittanning after more surveillance footage showed him yelling and acting aggressively toward a cashier while holding a blueberry muffin in one hand and a tactical knife in the other.

Aggregate charges of simple assault, public drunkenness, and harassment from the incidents were dropped when Paul agreed to undergo alcohol evaluation and anger management classes.

Paul was in a fight with himself and losing badly, and these slaps on the wrist could not prevent the inevitable.

On December 21, 2016, an iPhone Paul purchased as a Christmas present for Geno went missing. Despite Charlie's repeated denials, Paul knew Charlie was responsible. Charlie was always scavenging for money to score his next fix and had already been caught stealing and pawning Paul's diamond earrings and one of his expensive

A FALLEN STAR

watches. Paul understood Charlie could not help himself, but he could no longer stomach his lies – especially when Charlie was taking from one of his kids.

Paul was out drinking while Charlie and Annie were decorating his home for Christmas. He arrived later, barged through his front door, and stabbed Charlie in his upper thigh with a knife.

Neighbors heard the commotion and called 911. Charlie was waiting in the driveway when the police arrived. The smell of wine wafted from Paul's breath as he furiously paced back and forth on his porch and argued with his mother before turning his attention to the officers. He went inside and locked the door before he claimed police tricked him into gaining entrance, and he was tased. At one point, he assumed a boxing stance and challenged them to "a fair fight." After ignoring repeated commands, cops needed pepper spray to get him into handcuffs.

Paul alleged it got uglier from there. "They sucker-punched me," he said. "They Rodney-Kinged me on the front porch and beat the fuck outta me. I didn't have my arms, but I (fought back with) my legs."

He also went at them with his mouth. According to a felony complaint, Paul spat in the face of an officer and made threats against all of their lives, screaming, "Mom, get all their names. I know they have to live in the city. I'm gonna kill them."

Paul was finally subdued after medics arrived to fit him with a spit shield. He was arrested and jailed on four counts of aggravated assault, two counts of aggravated harassment by a prisoner, seven counts of terroristic threats, and one count of possessing an instrument of crime and simple assault. "(Paul) could be dangerous if he was fucked up and in a bad mood," Mike Kuster said.

"(Police) had to use mace and a stun gun on him, and it took five of them to hold him down."

The authorities took Paul to Allegheny County Jail and assigned him to a six-month inmate rehab program. The assault charges involving Annie and Charlie were dropped when neither appeared to testify at Paul's February 8, 2017, preliminary hearing. Paul moved into another halfway house that summer to serve additional time through a six-month, locked-down inpatient program as he awaited a non-jury trial for the charges levied by law enforcement.

He was embarrassed and wanted to put the ordeal behind him. He was on the ropes, struggling to keep his balance, wondering if he could make it to the bell.

And then his circumstances became unbearable.

"I knew I would eventually get a call from someone in my family that Charlie did the wrong thing and was dead," Paul said.

He just always assumed he had more time.

Charlie passed away on July 4 after overdosing on crack. Paul wept uncontrollably for weeks. "You can't do things like he did, to the excess that he did, because your body just can't handle it."

The hypocrisy was lost on Paul at the time as he drank even more excessively. Charlie was cremated. Paul kept his urn close by his side and talked to him daily. He would always joke that Charlie was crazy but call him the best person he ever knew.

Paul pleaded guilty on March 22, 2018, to simple assault on police and resisting arrest, was released on previous time served, and ordered to complete probation. Judge Manning addressed Paul harshly. "The court looks

A FALLEN STAR

at you like a real failure," he said. "A failure of yourself and a failure of us."

Manning warned Paul that any relapse would land him in state prison. Paul appeared remorseful but was secretly apathetic. Throughout the most challenging periods, he had always been able to see a light at the end of the tunnel.

Since retiring from his "TRUE LOVE," the words tattooed across his knuckles, he only saw darkness.

***

Nadine had already been married and separated when she decided to reconnect with Paul on Facebook. They had not spoken in several years, but she had read about Paul's problems on social media and had grown concerned about his mental health.

Paul replied to her post, and they began talking again. Nadine was in the throes of her own emotional meltdown, alleging she was sexually harassed by a former nightclub employer and bullied into quitting her job. Nadine and Paul consoled each other and found common ground. Their dynamic had always been messy, but Paul liked hearing Nadine's voice.

He also liked hearing the sounds of the gym. After training amateurs at WPAL Helman's Boxing Club in Punxsutawney, Paul told Nadine how much he adored volunteering his expertise alongside friends Lamar Williams and James Hoy at Third Avenue Boxing Gym and Teddy Mrkonja at the Gold Medal Boxing Club in Pittsburgh. It enabled him to share three decades of wisdom with underprivileged kids harboring dreams of becoming world champions.

Paul saw himself in their faces. Coaching came naturally, and it brought him happiness.

The rest of his days were a meaningless void filled with manual labor and beer. Paul woke up each morning at 5:30 a.m. to begin eight hours of back-breaking work with a tree removal service before punching out each afternoon to guzzle the cold ones he kept stocked in his fridge.

Thoughts of Charlie compelled him to get hammered. And when he learned Whitaker, his friend and idol, had been killed in the summer of 2019 after being struck by a car, he plummeted even further.

Nadine tried to stimulate Paul with updates about Geno. She had started her own laser treatment business and pushed Paul to explore his ambition of opening a boxing gym. As their communication ebbed and flowed through the first year of the COVID-19 pandemic, she realized she could never help him from Nevada.

Paul sank to his lowest in the winter of 2021 when Acri passed away following a two-and-a-half-year battle with pancreatic cancer. McCauley had privately shuttled Acri to his treatments, but no one else knew of his condition. "That fucked me up – it destroyed me," Paul said. "(Acri) didn't even tell anyone."

Despite their differences, Paul had made amends with his longtime promoter and credited him as one of the original reasons he became a champion. When Acri abruptly disappeared forever, like many loved ones before him, he questioned the point of continuing onward.

Paul resumed using heroin that summer. He overdosed twice, and paramedics needed Narcan to revive him.

Nadine had heard enough and decided to reappear in Paul's life. She flew to Pittsburgh with Geno that fall after Paul was inducted into the Pennsylvania Boxing Hall of Fame. They rented a car and drove five hours to the awards

A FALLEN STAR

ceremony in Philadelphia. The excursion, she hoped, would remind Paul of his significance to his family and the boxing community.

His priorities, however, were clear. "The whole way down, Paul kept drinking these mini bottles of liquor," she said. "I kept throwing them away at each stop, and then you'd see more. I'd swear he'd (somehow) keep buying them. I had never known anyone who liked drinking so much.

Paul was plastered when he arrived at The Bridgemen's Ballroom but equally charming. Clad in a plaid tie, khaki pants, and a baseball cap, he accepted his honorary plaque and delivered a heartfelt speech praising Annie, who made the trip separately, before walking off stage and hugging her. It was a memorable outing, even though strangers continued buying Paul cocktails, which would cause him to forget some details. "Paul is not the kind of person to have one drink at a time," Nadine said. "He's usually having someone bring him two drinks at a time."

She reasoned it would remain that way until he got help.

Paul reentered rehab in November 2021 and remained for more than two months. He graduated from the program with a new sense of optimism, but Nadine was too familiar with Paul's compulsive tendencies and knew a relapse was probable. She believed a full recovery could only be achieved when he fully removed himself from the bad influences that perpetually stood in his way.

As Paul continued to rekindle his relationship with Nadine, the only woman he had never stopped loving, he considered starting afresh with her in Las Vegas. And the more Geno spoke of becoming a professional boxer like his dad, the more appealing the idea became. It presented itself as a saving grace, a resolution that might finally stick.

But before taking a leap of faith, Paul resolved to teach Geno so much more. He had sidestepped thousands of punches through 51 fights and had been knocked out by only one opponent.

Himself.

"I should have never drank or done any drugs, period," Paul said.

He bowed his head and solemnly added, "It's a miracle that I'm still even here."

Chapter 12: The Last Round

Paul surveys the craftmanship of his 12-by-12-foot boxing ring the way an art connoisseur studies an exquisite painting. Its canvas floor is emblazoned with the letters "PK" in his signature scrawl. The initials also adorn the pads on each ring post, along with the emblem of his new training endeavor – "Spadafora Boxing" – and the logo of Nadine's holistic body lab.

The investment, funded by the sale of his Pennsylvania home, is the centerpiece of the cramped garage unit inside his suburban Las Vegas residence and comes accessorized with mirrored walls, punching bags, weights, an elliptical machine, an exercise bike, and a treadmill. It is here, in this makeshift training facility, that Paul continues to work with fighters of all skill levels. "This is the only thing I know how to do to help people," he says. "I can no longer help people any other way. I used to be able to give them money to get them out of their problem, and I don't have money to give them anymore. I can still help (people), and this is a way I can help them – right in here."

To be truly useful, Paul understands the need to improve from within. And since touching down in the desert during the summer of 2022, he knows there will never be any shortcuts to achieving success, or in his case, sobriety.

He initially hoped a busy itinerary would keep him in line. After reuniting with Reid, who had been coaching Geno, Paul trained his son and several of Reid's fighters at DLX Boxing Gym.

He was pursuing his new passion, putting money in his pocket, and feeling good.

Within months, he began cutting the water bottles he brought to the gym with red wine. Paul fooled himself into thinking he was making a reasonable allowance and fooled others by continuing to function reasonably.

During a podcast appearance on *ThaBoxingVoice*, Paul chose his words judiciously when probed about the six rounds he went with Floyd Mayweather Jr. and provided a humble assessment of the hysteria surrounding the video, which had become legendary.

Privately, he still contemplated the plausibility of boxing Mayweather in an exhibition bout and finally achieving closure.

Paul stole an opening to broach the subject with Mayweather at Resorts World Casino that August during the 2022 Nevada Boxing Hall of Fame Gala. He was there with Nadine to support Roy Jones Jr., who was being inducted alongside Mayweather, but knew he would regret passing up the opportunity to verbalize his request in person.

After lubricating himself with several Jack-and-Cokes, Paul snaked through Mayweather's security team and, with seconds to spare, congratulated his lifelong nemesis with a cordial hug before asking him for a fight. Paul was pushed away before he could solicit any response and was told that same evening he would "get his ass whupped" when he made the same inquiry to Floyd Sr.

Nadine vehemently discouraged Paul from consuming alcohol, especially when a CAT scan revealed the early signs of chronic traumatic encephalopathy (CTE), a brain disorder Paul believes was triggered by damage withstood late in his boxing career.

It became impossible, no less, to maintain constant surveillance. The nights became particularly nerve-racking when Paul's drinking accelerated the following spring and led to drug use. "It was a tough time for my dad," Geno says. "When he would get (drunk) like that, he would get super unpredictable. Anything could happen that could cause serious problems."

This danger was realized in the early morning of May 31, 2023, when Paul barged into the house after smoking crystal methamphetamine. He had angrily walked several miles without his shirt and shoes and had no memory of where he had left his newly purchased Harley Davidson motorcycle. He rambled room-to-room with a baseball bat and destroyed everything in his sight.

Nadine made a tearful phone call to the police, and the local SWAT Team was needed to remove Paul from the premises.

He was arrested on aggravated assault charges and remained livid when released from jail a few days later, but only with himself. Paul moved across the country to become a different man, but the only thing that changed was his zip code. "(Paul) is fighting the biggest fight of his life now," says Horn, "except it's not for a belt or a paycheck."

Paul checked himself into an addiction treatment center called Vegas Stronger and reemerged a month later with a prescription for Dilsufiram. The tablet is ingested daily and prohibits alcohol from metabolizing in his body.

A single drop can cause him severe illness. "I wouldn't trust myself if I didn't take it," Paul says.

He instead puts all of his trust in his family, which has been encouraging his progress every step of the way. Paul has remained clean and sober since early summer. It is his longest stretch since he was a teenager and a breakthrough that is not lost on Harry.

After briefly returning to the ring and improving to 3-0 as a pro middleweight in 2000, Harry retired a second time and opened his own concrete company. He remarried and is the proud father of three sons and two daughters.

He is also proud of his own sobriety, which is approaching the 20-year milestone. Harry only hopes Paul continues down a similar path. "I wish for him to continue to stay sober," he says. "If he does, everything else will fall into place."

Paul sees it happening with his mother. Annie's struggle with drugs persisted until she entered rehab last year and finally got clean. Although she never realized her childhood aspiration of joining a convent, Annie now lives in an assisted living facility operated exclusively by nuns.

She remains a feisty old bird at 72 but will always have a soft spot for her middle child and his pursuit of happiness.

And that is all Paul wishes for Geno. Reid believes Geno (13-3) has the potential to one day surpass Paul's boxing accomplishments when he turns pro. Paul would like nothing more but ultimately wants Geno to succeed in whatever he does.

Geno is simply content to have his father again. "It's way better for him to be here with us, obviously," he says. "We have a great relationship. I love my dad, and we always hang out. I get to see my mom happy all the time now, so that's good, too."

Paul and Nadine finally wed on September 30, 2023, in the Mediterranean coastal town of Maratea, Italy. Since their ceremony was held under the statue of Christ the Redeemer, it was almost as if Paul was also being *baptized* a new man. They shared an inside laugh as a violinist captured the moment with an eloquent rendition of "Beauty and the Beast."

"Nadine is my real-life Wonder Woman that I now get to be with forever," he says before joking, "Love always wins, and our love is bulletproof."

With his new wife officially by his side, Paul continues to grow his brand as a trainer. He takes in new fighters weekly while also developing The Spadafora Boxing Foundation, a non-profit organization that provides training, travel, equipment, and housing to help underprivileged athletes pursue their dreams in the ring. "If I don't volunteer this type of knowledge I have to share, it would be a sin," he says.

Similarly, Paul could never forgive himself if he ignored his other obligations. He intends to become more involved in his daughters' lives and positively influence his youngest son, Paul Jr., now 7. Nadine expresses optimism that he will return to his writing and reconnect with God.

Paul knows people expect him to fail but remains content living out his remaining days in a gambler's paradise and will always bet on himself. He pledges to keep fighting.

It is what Pecora would have wanted.

"It ain't over till it's over," Paul says enthusiastically. "That's the way it was with me in boxing. That's how it is in my life right now. You gotta keep going, even when you get tired and want to give up."

The smile dissipates as he pauses to consider the bigger picture.

"If you keep working and keep trying to do the right thing, things will get better. You just always gotta believe that."

Notes

This biography pulls heavily from the author's transcripts of interviews conducted with Paul Spadafora, his family members, managers, and trainers, and observations of footage from numerous fights.

Ch. 1 – Sin City Salvation
Lidz, Franz. "Staying Power Though Lacking a Knockout Punch, Lightweight Paul Spadafora Thrives on Guile and Determination." SI.com. Sports Illustrated, May 26, 2003. https://vault.si.com/vault/2003/05/26/staying-power-though-lacking-a-knockout-punch-lightweight-paul-spadafora-thrives-on-guile-and-determination.

Scarnati, Chris. "Chris Scarnati: Finally Sober and Still Undefeated, Spadafora Hopes for Mayweather Shot." SI.com. Sports Illustrated, April 5, 2013. http://www.si.com/mma/2013/04/05/ paul-spadafora-boxer-comeback.

Kane, Karen. "Former Boxing Champ Spadafora Charged with AssaultingWoman, 63, in Crafton Bar." Post-Gazette.com, April 7, 2016. http://www.post- gazette.com/local/city/2016/04/07/Former-IBF-boxing-champ-Paul-Spadafora-charged-with-assaulting-63-year-old-woman-in-Crafton-Pittsburgh-bar/stories/201604070199.

wms702. "Paul Spadafora vs Hector Velasquez (Full Fight)." YouTube, March 26, 2016. https://www.youtube.com/watch?v=vJ1vzjDLlWs.

Ch. 2 – Unfortunate Son
Commonwealth of Pennsylvania vs. *NAME REDACTED* (Court of Common Pleas of Allegheny County December 3, 1981).

Ch. 3 – Road from Perdition
"Billy Conn." BoxRec. Accessed November 27, 2022. https://boxrec.com/en/box-pro/9007.

"Frank Klaus." BoxRec. Accessed November 27, 2022. https://boxrec.com/en/box-pro/11285.

"George Chip." BoxRec. Accessed November 27, 2022. https://boxrec.com/en/box-pro/11253.

Notes

"Harry Greb." BoxRec. Accessed November 27, 2022. https://boxrec.com/en/box-pro/9019.

Toledo, Springs. *Smokestack Lightning: Harry Greb, 1919*. Boston, Massachusetts: Self-Published, 2019.

Cavanaugh, Douglas. *Pittsburgh Boxing: A Pictorial History*. Pittsburgh, Pennsylvania: Self-Published, 2020.

"Teddy Yarosz." BoxRec. Accessed November 27, 2022. https://boxrec.com/en/box-pro/10519.

"Sammy Angott." BoxRec. Accessed November 27, 2022. https://boxrec.com/en/box-pro/9624.

"Fritzie Zivic." BoxRec. Accessed November 27, 2022. https://boxrec.com/en/box-pro/9437.

Joe Louis - Billy Conn Documentary ("Battle Lines"). YouTube. ESPN Classic, 2011. https://www.youtube.com/watch?v=XWDsRsqCy8o.

McHugh, Roy. *When Pittsburgh Was a Fight Town*. Pittsburgh, Pennsylvania: Self-Published, 2019.

Ch. 4 – P.K.'s Prodigy

"Past Champions 90's." Pagolden.com. http://www.pagoldengloves.com/past-champions.

"US National Golden Gloves - Milwaukee - April 18-23, 1994." http://amateur-boxing.strefa.pl/Nationalchamps/USGoldenGloves1994.html.

"Key Dates and Events in Paul Spadafora's Life." *Pittsburgh Post-Gazette*, November 3, 2003.

Ch. 5 – Ballrooms and Boxing Gloves

"Paul Spadafora." BoxRec. Accessed November 27, 2022. https://boxrec.com/en/box-pro/6517.

PAUL SPADAFORA VS MICHAEL LOPEZ (20-02-1996). BitChute. USA Network Tuesday Night Fights, 2020. http://www.bitchute.com/video/vlYG3sg1ORZq/.

"Paul Spadafora." BoxRec. Accessed November 27, 2022. https://boxrec.com/en/box-pro/6517.

Ch. 6 – Coronation of a King

"Paul Spadafora." BoxRec. Accessed November 27, 2022. https://boxrec.com/en/box-pro/6517.

Notes

Hirsley, Michael. "Two local fighters lose main bouts on ESPN2 card." Chicago Tribune, January 23, 1999. http://www.chicagotribune.com/news/ct-xpm-1999-01-23-9901230104-story.html.

Finder, Chuck. "TV Analyst -- Yes, That Analyst -- Now Flips for Champion Spadafora." Post-Gazette.com, December 16, 1999. http://old.post-gazette.com/tv/19991216thebig.asp.

"Paul Spadafora." BoxRec. Accessed November 27, 2022. https://boxrec.com/en/box-pro/6517.

Price, Terry. "Cardona Loses His Advantage ." www.courant.com. Hartford Courant, July 31, 1999. https://www.courant.com/1999/07/31/cardona-loses-his- advantage-boxing-terry-price/.

"Israel Cardona." BoxRec. Accessed November 27, 2022. https://boxrec.com/en/box-pro/6435.

"Leonard Dorin." BoxRec. Accessed November 27, 2022. https://boxrec.com/en/box-pro/14354.

Paul Spadafora Vs Pito Cardona Rds 1 2 & Prefight. YouTube. USA: ESPN Friday Night Fights, 1999. https://www.youtube.com/watch?v=q6FCr8niL98&t=5s.

Paul Spadafora Vs Pito Cardona Rds 3, 4, 5, 6. YouTube. ESPN Friday Night Fights, 2011. https://www.youtube.com/watch?v=a6ijtXLIL14&t=127s.

Paul Spadafora Vs Pito Cardona Rds 7, 8, 9, 10. YouTube. ESPN Friday Night Fights, 2011. https://www.youtube.com/watch?v=H7w3YSQ076g&t=3s.

Paul Spadafora Vs Pito Cardona Rds 11, 12 & Postfight. YouTube. ESPN Friday Night Fights, 2011. https://www.youtube.com/watch?v=dX-MbdY4SII.

Finder, Chuck. "Obituary: Eugene Polecritti / champion's grandfather came home to die." Post-Gazette.com, June 26, 2001. https://old.postgazette.com/obituaries/20010626 polecritti0626p2.asp.

Wainwright, Anson. "Best I Trained: Jesse Reid." The Ring, January 4, 2022. https://www.ringtv.com/632837-best-i-trained-jesse-reid/.

"Jesse Reid's Lessons, and the Man Who Beat Floyd Mayweather Jr.." VICE, July 26, 2016. https://www.vice.com/en/article/aeb3pk/jesse-reids-lessons-and-the-man-who-beat-floyd-mayweather-jr.

Notes

"Paul Spadafora vs Floyd Mayweather Jr. (Enhanced Footage | Rounds 1,2,3 - Part 1 of 2)." YouTube. YouTube, February 1, 2016. https://www.youtube. com/watch?v=gzYJDb8RbL8.

"Paul Spadafora vs Floyd Mayweather Jr. (Enhanced Footage | Rounds 4,5,6 - Part 2 of 2)." YouTube. YouTube, February 1, 2016. https://www.youtube.com /watch?v=Qc2x5s2Yulc.

Ch. 7 – The Fourth Franchise

Finder, Chuck. "Spadafora a Cut Above." *Pittsburgh Post-Gazette*. December 18, 1999.

"Spadafora Retains IBF Lightweight Title, Remains Unbeaten." ESPN.com.://a.espncdn.com/boxing/news/1999/1217/239457.html.

Paul Spadafora vs Victoriano Sosa - 1/4. YouTube. ESPN2 Friday Night Fights, 2011. https://www.youtube.com/watch?v=nAksUhNTu_8.

Paul Spadafora vs Victoriano Sosa - 2/4. YouTube. ESPN2 Friday Night Fights, 2011. https://www.youtube.com/watch?v=xETQqkJ-wzo.

Paul Spadafora vs Victoriano Sosa - 3/4. YouTube. ESPN2 Friday Night Fights, 2011. https://www.youtube.com/watch?v=19TNrUsGDzY.

Paul Spadafora vs Victoriano Sosa - 4/4.YouTube. ESPN2 Friday Night Fights, 2011. https://www.youtube.com/watch?v=TWjMFJYJueo.

Finder, Chuck. "Spadafora went south to find some direction." Post-Gazette.com, May 5, 2000. https://old.post-gazette.com/sports_headlines/20000505fite4.asp.

Paul Spadafora vs Mike Griffith - HBO KO Nation May 6, 2000. YouTube. HBO KO Nation, 2022. https://www.youtube.com/watch?v=LcwYn9syK58.

Finder, Chuck. "Spadafora retains IBF belt after controversial decision over Griffith." Post-Gazette.com, May 7, 2000. http://old.post-gazette.com/ sports_headlines/20000507fite1.asp.

"Key Dates and Events in Paul Spadafora's Life." Post-Gazette.com, November 2, 2003. https://www.post-gazette.com/sports/other-sports/2003/11/02/Key-dates-and-events-in-Paul-Spadafora-s-life/stories/200311020093.

Finder, Chuck. "Spadafora Gets Back to Basics in Victory over Jones." *Pittsburgh Post-Gazette*. September 10, 2000.

Notes

Finder, Chuck. "Spadafora devours Rulli's words." Post-Gazette.com, December 15, 2000. http://old.post-gazette.com/sports/other/20001215fite1.asp.

Paul Spadafora vs Billy Irwin - HBO KO Nation December 16, 2000. YouTube. HBO KO Nation, 2020. https://www.youtube.com/watch?v=v CDcnK99uXs&t=5s.

Finder, Chuck. "Spadafora's Form Returns as He Scores a Unanimous Decision." *Pittsburgh Post-Gazette*. December 17, 2000.

"Joel Perez." BoxRec. Accessed November 28, 2022. https://boxrec.com/en/box-pro/6992.

Gorman, Kevin. "Spadafora to Defend IBF Lightweight Title Tonight against Perez." Triblive.com, March 8, 2001.https://archive.triblive.com/news/spadafora-to-defend-ibf-lightweight-title-tonight-against-perez/.

Paul Spadafora vs Joel Perez [10-05-2001]. YouTube. ESPN2 Tuesday Night Fights, 2020. https://www.youtube.com/watch?v=2WJHwyUCdpk.

Gorman, Kevin. "Spadafora Retains Title." Triblive.com, Match 9, 2001. https://archive.triblive.com/news/spadafora-retains-title/.

"Charles Tschorniawsky." BoxRec. Accessed November 28, 2022. https://boxrec.com/en/box-pro/9049.

Robinson, Edward G. "Name Game Threatens Spadafora." Post-Gazette.com, August 14, 2001. https://old.postgazette.com/sports/other/20010814spadafora0814np3.asp.

Cipriano, Guy. "Spadafora Easily Defends Title." Triblive.com, August 15, 2001. https://archive.triblive.com/news/spadafora-easily-defends-title/.

Fittipaldo, Ray. "Spadafora Tops Tschorniawsky." *Pittsburgh Post-Gazette*. August 15, 2001.

Ch. 8 – Confluence of Chaos

"Angel Manfredy." BoxRec. Accessed November 28, 2022.https://boxrec.com/en/box-pro/5180.

Hoffer, Richard. " Hell's Angel." *Sports Illustrated*, December 7, 1998.

Wainwright, Anson. "Best I Faced: Angel Manfredy." The Ring, August 28, 2018. https://www.ringtv.com/542433-best-i-faced-angel-manfredy/.

Notes

Robinson, Edward G. "Clean and Sober, Manfredy a Dangerous Foe for Spadafora." Post-Gazette.com, March 6, 2002. http://old.post-gazette.com/sports/other/20020306 manfredy0306p5.asp.
Paul Spadafora vs Angel Manfredy - HBO Boxing After Dark March 9, 2002. YouTube. HBO Boxing After Dark, 2022. https://www.youtube.com/watch?v=BDYVMngvYrQ.
Gorman, Kevin. "Spadafora ready to defend IBF title." Triblive.com, October 1, 2002. https://archive.triblive.com/news/spadafora-ready-to-defend-ibf-title/.
Jose Luis Castillo vs Floyd Mayweather Jr I April 20, 2002. YouTube. HBO World Championship Boxing, 2021. https://www.youtube.com/watch?v=mHgxRIr-hpA.
Silver, Jonathan D. "Spadafora Posts Bail for Drug Suspect." Post-Gazette.com, August 16, 2002. http://old.post-gazette.com/neigh_west/20020816spadafora5.asp.
PAUL SPADAFORA vs. DENNIS HOLBAEK | FULL FIGHT | BOXING WORLD WEEKLY. YouTube. Boxing World Weekly, 2021. https://www.youtube.com/ watch?v=VkMvuZEBQhM&t=161s.
Finder, Chuck. "Spadafora Rallies to Score Decision against Holbaek." *Pittsburgh Post-Gazette*. November 10, 2022.
Gorman, Kevin. "Spadafora Ready for Dorin." Triblive.com, May 1, 2003. https://archive.triblive.com/news/spadafora-ready-for-dorin/.
Chuck, Finder. "Spadafora Escapes to Remote Area of Washington County to Prepare for His Title Unification Bout." Post-Gazette.com, May 11, 2003. https://old.post-gazette.com/sports/other/20030511spadafora0511p3.asp.
Finder, Chuck. "Prefight sparring is between the handlers, not Spadafora, Dorin." Post-Gazette.com, May 16, 2003. http://old.post-gazette.com/sports/other/20030516 spadaforasptother2p2.asp.
2003 05 17 Leonard Dorin vs Paul Spadafora. YouTube. HBO Boxing After Dark, 2018. https://www.youtube.com/watch?v=iInGPKF6z_U.
Finder, Chuck. "Expect Spadafora-Dorin Rematch." *Pittsburgh Post-Gazette*, May 19, 2003.
Gorman, Kevin. "Spadafora Relinquishes IBF Title." Triblive.com, June 27, 2003. https://archive.triblive.com/news/spadafora-relinquishes-ibf-title-2/.

Ch. 9 – Loaded and Dangerous

Notes

Scarnati, Chris. "Chris Scarnati: Finally Sober and Still Undefeated, Spadafora Hopes for Mayweather Shot." Sports Illustrated, April 5, 2013. http://www.si.com/mma/2013/04/05/ paul-spadafora-boxer-comeback.

Roebuck, Karen. "Boxer Charged in Girlfriend's Shooting." Triblive.com, October 27, 2003. https://archive.triblive.com/news/boxer-charged-in-girlfriends-shooting/.

Rotstein, Gary. "Boxer Spadafora Arrested in Shooting." *Pittsburgh Post-Gazette*, October 27, 2003.

Simonich, Milan. "Spadafora Held for Trial." Post-Gazette.com, November 11, 2003. https://old.postgazette.com/localnews/20031111spadafora1111p3.asp.%C2%A0126

May, Glenn. "Spadafora Faces Trial for Shooting." Triblive.com, November 11, 2003. https://archive.triblive.com/news/spadafora-faces-trial-for-shooting/.

Heltzel, Bill. "Witnesses dispute Spadafora's shooting story." Post-Gazette.com, October 28, 2003. https://old.post-gazette.com/localnews/20031028spadaforaloc2.asp.

Commonwealth of Pennsylvania vs. Paul Spadafora (Court of Common Pleas of Allegheny County October 27, 2003).

Heltzel, Bill. "Witnesses dispute Spadafora's shooting story." Post-Gazette.com, October 28, 2003. https://old.post-gazette.com/localnews/20031028spadaforaloc2.asp.

May, Glenn. "Spadafora Faces Trial for Shooting." Triblive.com, November 11, 2003. https://archive.triblive.com/news/spadafora-faces-trial-for-shooting/.

Simonich, Milan. "Spadafora Held for Trial." Post-Gazette.com, November 11, 2003. https://old.post-gazette.com/localnews/20031111spadafora1111p3.asp.

"Paul Spadafora." BoxRec. Accessed November 27, 2022. https://boxrec.com/en/box-pro/6517.

Bendel, Joe. "Campos out to Ruin Spadafora's Night." Triblive.com, July 17, 2004. https://archive.triblive.com/news/campos-out-to-ruin-spadaforas-night/.

Finder, Chuck. "Spadafora Manages TKO in Final Round." *Pittsburgh Post-Gazette*, July 18, 2004.

Notes

McKinnon, Jim. "Spadafora on House Arrest after Weekend Incident." Post-Gazette.com, September 7, 2004. https://www.post-gazette.com /breaking/2004/09/07/Spadafora-on-house-arrest-after-weekend-incident/stories/200409070168.

Hasch, Michael. "Boxer Spadafora in Jail after Bond Revoked." Triblive.com. Pittsburgh Tribune-Review, December 11, 2004. https://archive.triblive.com/news/boxer-spadafora-in-jail-after-bond-revoked/.

McKinnon, Jim. "Boxer Spadafora Violates Judge's Order, Back in Jail." Post-Gazette.com, December 11, 2004. https://www.postgazette.com/local/west/2004/12/11/ Boxer-Spadafora-violates-judge-s-order-back-in-jail/stories/200412110183.

May, Glenn. "Spadafora's Toughest Count: Up to 17 Years." Triblive.com, December 21, 2004. https://archive.triblive.com/news/spadaforas-toughest-count-up-to-17-years/.

Hamill, Sean D. "After Hitting Bottom, Trying to Regain the Top." NYTimes.com, June 21, 2009. https://www.nytimes.com/2009/06/22/sports/22boxer.html.

Harlan, Chico. "Boxing: Can Spadafora Rebound from Rock Bottom?" *Pittsburgh Post-Gazette*, February 27, 2005.

Ch. 10 – The Second Act

Hamill, Sean D. "Body Language." https://www.pghcitypaper.com, December 17, 2009. https://www.pghcitypaper.com/news/body-language-1343032.

Gorman, Kevin. "Spadafora Gets New Cutman." Triblive.com. Pittsburgh Tribune-Review, July 14, 2004. https://archive.triblive.com/news/spadafora-gets-new-cut-man/.

"Zepeda Looks to Retire Spadafora." BoxingScene.com. BoxingScene, November 2, 2006. https://www.boxingscene.com/zepeda-looks-retire-spadafora--6064?print_friendly=1.

"Oisin 'Gael Force' Fagan to Face Paul Spadafora, March 9 ." boxing247.com. East Side Boxing, February 19, 2007. https://www.boxing247.com/weblog/archives/ 112400.

Oisin Fagan - Paul Spadafora Rounds 1-2. YouTube. Fox Sports Networks, 2008. https://www.youtube.com/watch?v=voTAZv4VIhU.

Notes

Oisin Fagan - Paul Spadafora Rounds 3-4. YouTube. Fox Sports Network, 2008. https://www.youtube.com/watch?v=7Tk2L7QLPRs.
Oisin Fagan - Paul Spadafora Rounds 8-9. YouTube. Fox Sports Network, 2008. https://www.youtube.com/watch?v=JcKqIi2TcR8.
Oisin Fagan - Paul Spadafora Round 10. YouTube. Fox Sports Network, 2008. https://www.youtube.com/watch?v=yz1ThJYbOt0&t=4s.
Gorman, Kevin. "'Pittsburgh Kid' Spadafora Squares up for Comeback." Triblive.com. Pittsburgh Tribune-Review, August 10, 2008. https://archive.triblive.com/news/pittsburgh-kid-spadafora-squares-up-for- comeback-2/.
Cato, Jason. "35 Charged in Drug Ring in City's Southern Neighborhoods." Triblive.com. Pittsburgh Tribune-Review, November 20, 2008. https://archive.triblive.com/news/35-charged-in-drug-ring-in-citys-southern-neighborhoods/.
DiRienzo, Dominick. "Spadafora Stays Unbeaten in Comeback Bout." Meadvilletribune.com. Meadville Tribune, April 28, 2008. https://www.meadvilletribune.com/archives/spadafora-stays-unbeaten-in-comeback-bout/article_8774bd63-6007-5bb5-84ad-a9e6f3ace1f8.html.
Erie Boxing. *2008 Erie Boxing - Paul Spadafora - Shad Howard (Round 1-8). YouTube.* USA: Erie Boxing, 2008. https://www.youtube.com/watch?v=lDRo-2AoC24.
Miller, Ed. "In His Prime, Pernell Whitaker Was Hampton Roads' Own Professional Franchise." Pilotonline.com, July 15, 2019. https://www. pilotonline.com/sports/article_e3711620 a72d-11e9-8640-9b1aa3e1180a.html.
Wainwright, Anson. "Pernell Whitaker's Greatest Hits: The Sweetest Victories." The Ring, April 2, 2020. https://www.ringtv.com/595938-pernell-whitakers-greatest-hits-the-sweetest victories/.
Zeise, Paul. "Spadafora Wins by TKO." Gazette, June 24, 2009. https://www.post-gazette.com/breaking/2009/06/24/Spadafora-wins-by-TKO/stories/200906240207.
Davenport, Gary. "Ranking the Top 10 Defenses in NFL History." Bleacher Report, June 20, 2019. https://bleacherreport.com/articles/2841622-ranking-the-top-10-defenses-in-nfl-history.
Ogilvie, Kenneth W. "Spadafora Decisions White over Eight at Heinz Field." New Pittsburgh Courier, October 8, 2009.

Notes

https://newpittsburghcourier.com /2009/10/08/spadafora decisions-white-over-eight-at-heinz-field/.
Associated Press. "Spadafora Still Unbeaten, Stops Fiorletta in 8th Round." New Pittsburgh Courier, March 24, 2010. https://newpittsburghcourier.com/2010/ 03/24/spadafora-still-unbeaten-stops-fiorletta-in-8th-round/.
Stradley, Don. *Berserk*. Boston, MA: Hamilcar Publications, 2019.
Gorman, Kevin. "Spadafora Done Ballroom Dancing." Triblive.com, November 20, 2010. https://archive.triblive.com/news/gorman-spadafora-done-ballroom-dancing/.
"Paul Spadafora – OTR Episodes: 106." On The Ropes Boxing Radio, January 5, 2011. https://ontheropesboxing.com/about/paulspadafora/.
Floyd Mayweather Jr vs DeMarcus Corley May 22, 2004. *YouTube*. HBO World Championship Boxing, 2021. https://www.youtube.com/watch?v =ALnuHm2YfoY.
Floyd Mayweather Jr. vs Zab Judah. *YouTube*. Top Rank Boxing, 2022. https://www.youtube.com/watch?v=dXq8P_37lMg.
Chiappetta, Mike. "The Myth of Floyd Mayweather's Southpaw Struggles." MMA Fighting, August 25, 2017. https://www.mmafighting.com/2017/8/25/ 16183288/the-myth-of-floyd-mayweathers-southpaw-struggles.
SI Staff. "Mayweather Confirms Sept. 17 Fight with Victor Ortiz – Sports Illustrated." www.SportsIllustrated.com, June 7, 2011. https://www.si.com /boxing/2011/06/07/mayweather-ortiz.
Scarnati, Chris. "Chris Scarnati: Finally Sober and Still Undefeated, Spadafora Hopes for Mayweather Shot." Sports Illustrated, April 5, 2013. http://www.si.com/mma/2013/04/05/ paul-spadafora-boxer-comeback.
"Tom Yankello's World Class Boxing Gym Bio." WorldClassBoxingGym. Accessed June 30, 2023. https://www.worldclassboxinggym.com/bio.
"Humberto Toledo." BoxRec. Accessed June 30, 2023. https://boxrec.com/en/box-pro/188490.
Brandolph, Adam. "Ex-Manager Hits Boxer Spadafora with Lawsuit." Triblive.com, September 26, 2012. https://archive.triblive.com/news/ex-manager-hits-boxer-spadafora-with-lawsuit/.
Gorman, Kevin. "Spadafora Wins 1st Fight after 20-Month Layoff." Triblive.com, August 18, 2012. https://archive.triblive.com/sports/us-world/spadafora-wins-1st-fight-after-20-month-layoff/.

Notes

Brandolph, Adam. "Ex-Manager Hits Boxer Spadafora with Lawsuit." Triblive.com, September 26, 2012. https://archive.triblive.com/news/ex-manager-hits-boxer-spadafora-with-lawsuit/.

WBO. "Spadafora vs. Egberime on Saturday, December 1st in Chester, West Virginia." wboboxing.com, November 29, 2012. https://wboboxing.com/boxing-news/oriental-news/spadafora-vs-egberime-on-saturday-december-1st-in-chester-west-virginia/.

"Solomon Egberime." BoxRec.com. Accessed July 22, 2023. https://boxrec.com/en/proboxer/59599.

Paul Spadafora vs Solomon Egberime (Full Fight). YouTube. TNT Promotions, 2016. https://www.youtube.com/watch?v=evvQ74mQFLY.

"Spadafora: 'I Can't Change the Past, I Can Change My Future.'" foxness.com, March 13, 2013. https://www.foxnews.com/sports/spadafora-i-cant-change-the-past-i-can-change-my-future.amp.

Gorman, Kevin. "Spadafora Wins NABF Super Lightweight Belt." Triblive.com, April 6, 2013. https://archive.triblive.com/sports/other-local/spadafora-wins-nabf-super-lightweight-belt/.

Deitch, Charlie. "Spadafora Camp Refutes Claim That the Fighter 'Passed' on Nationally-Televised Fight." pghcitypaper.com, June 28, 2013. https://www.pghcitypaper.com/Blogh/archives/2013/06/28/spadafora-camp-refutes-claim-that-the-fighter-passed-on-nationally-televised-fight.

"Johan Perez." BoxRec. Accessed July 29, 2023. https://boxrec.com/en/box-pro/294852.

Paul Spadafora vs Johan Perez Full Fight Video! YouTube. World Class Boxing Channel, 2023. https://www.youtube.com/watch?v=bcYLwz_dLW0.

Paul Spadafora loses first fight. WPXI. WPXI, 2013. https://www.wpxi.com/news/local/perez hands-spadafora-first-defeat-wba-title-fight/289321660/.

Ch. 11 – A Fallen Star
Sager, Joe. "Streak behind Him, Spadafora Can Return Focus on a Title." Timesonline.com, July 11, 2014. https://www.timesonline.com/story/sports/2014/07/11/ streak-behind-him-spadafora-can/18485050007/.

Notes

Satterfield, Lem. "Paul Spadafora Could Sign with Golden Boy." The Ring, December 19, 2013. https://www.ringtv.com/182635-paul-spadafora-could-sign-with-golden-boy/.

"Hector Velazquez." BoxRec. Accessed August 1, 2023. https://boxrec.com/en/box-pro/7879.

Paul Spadafora vs Hector Velasquez (Full Fight). YouTube. TNT Promotions, 2016. https://www.youtube.com/watch?v=vJ1vzjDLlWs.

Danny Garcia–Rod Salk highlights. YouTube. Boxing Highlights, 2022. https:// www.youtube.com/watch?v=S5I9HCBMyWk.

Paul Spadafora now training with Kenny and Shawn Porter in Las Vegas. YouTube. Hustle Boss, 2014. https://www.youtube.com/watch?v=dX5vD_zsAFA.

Paul Spadafora sparring Devin Haney. YouTube. Tha Boxing Voice, 2014. https://www.youtube.com/watch?v=Wx3KQHCjfJo.

Oliver, Jeff. "Spadafora added to Vasquez-Lartey card." Triblive.com, March 6, 2015. https://archive.triblive.com/sports/other-local/spadafora-added-to-vasquez-lartey-card/.

Southpaw. Netflix, 2022. https://www.netflix.com/title/80038447.

"Caught on Camera: Witnesses Say Boxer Paul Spadafora Assaulted Woman at Bar." CBS News, April 7, 2016. https://www.cbsnews.com/pittsburgh/news/caught-on-video-witnesses-say-boxer-paul-spadafora-assaulted-woman-at-bar/.

"Boxer Accused of Terrorizing Sheetz Store While Holding Blueberry Muffin, Tactical Knife." CBS News, April 14, 2016. https://www.cbsnews.com/pittsburgh/news/ boxer-accused-of-terrorizing-sheetz-with-blueberry-muffin-tactical-knife/.

Sykes, Katelyn. "'Do the Right Thing:' Spadafora to Take Classes after Fracas with Woman at Bar." WTAE, March 1, 2021. https://www.wtae.com/article/do-the-right-thing-spadafora-to-take-classes-after-fracas-with-woman-at-bar/7480186#.

Guza, Megan. "Police: Boxer Paul Spadafora Stabbed Brother, Fought with Officers." Triblive.com, December 22, 2016. https://archive.triblive.com/local /pittsburgh-allegheny/police-boxer-paul-spadafora-stabbed-brother-fought-with-officers/.

"Assault Charges Involving Family Dropped against Boxer Paul Spadafora." CBS News, February 8, 2017. https://www.cbsnews.com/pittsburgh/news/paul-spadafora-stabbing-hearing/.

Notes

Ward, Paula Reed. "Ex-Boxer Paul Spadafora Pleads Guilty in 2016 Domestic Dispute." Post-Gazette.com, March 22, 2018. https://www.post-gazette.com/local/city/2018/03/22/Paul-Spadafora-assault-resisting-arrest-Pittsburgh-police-officers-domestic-violence/stories/201803220147.

Ch. 12 – The Final Round
Paul Spadafora congratulating Floyd Mayweather at Nevada Hall of Fame. YouTube, 2022.
https://www.youtube.com/shorts/CY05LSDYSjc.
Paul Spadafora asking Floyd Sr. to give him an exhibition with Floyd Mayweather. YouTube,
2022. https://www.youtube.com/shorts/Muzk7B6a3w4.

Acknowledgments

I am first and foremost thankful that Paul Spadafora allowed me to share his story. He welcomed me into his home with open arms and treated me like an old buddy. Paul pulled no punches during each interview and shared candid tales that were *so damned riveting*. I'll miss the spirited chats I shared with him over iced mochas, but I also look forward to seeing what he'll accomplish in the next chapter of his life. I wish Paul luck with his sobriety and pray he will make good choices.

A special thanks goes to Paul's mother, Annie, and older brother, Harry. Both added flesh to the bones of an already compelling narrative. I am incredibly grateful for Paul's wife, Nadine Spadafora, who tirelessly made herself available to hunt down photos and clarify ambiguous details. She is this book's MVP.

This biography wouldn't have been possible without the assistance of Paul's former trainers, Tom Yankello and Jesse Reid, manager Al McCauley, and promoter Roy Jones Jr., who graciously carved time out of their busy schedules to answer questions. It benefitted exceedingly from the commentary of boxing historian Douglas Cavanaugh, sports psychologist Dr. Adam Gallenberg, former TNT Promotions matchmaker Mark Yankello, and attorneys Mark Haak and Joe Horn. I appreciate their patience and professionalism.

I'm eternally indebted to Daniel Edwards of Creative Text Publishers for taking a chance on my manuscript and making me a first-time author. Dan made this project a lot of fun, and I look forward to working with him on future assignments.

Brian Fontenot, David McElhinny, Brian Gottesman, and Josh Gloer deserve considerable credit for combing through each page and suggesting essential edits. They are tremendous writers and even better friends.

Fighting Till the End was further enriched by the insight of former *Pittsburgh Post-Gazette* scribe and fellow Mizzou grad Chuck Finder and the skilled reporting of Kevin Gorman from the *Pittsburgh Tribune-Review*. Both captured the sights, sounds, and emotions from Paul's most significant fights. They are excellent journalists and the true curators of Paul's history.

To the teachers and administrators at Sto-Rox School District – thank you for taking an interest in a project about one of our former students. I'd also like to recognize Cara Reinard, a best-selling author from the northern Pittsburgh area who helped me recover my stolen laptop at the Gibsonia Starbucks. You restored my faith in the kindness of strangers.

Through it all, I've been blessed with a supportive family. My father and first editor (Jim), mother and fellow literary enthusiast (Mitzi), father- and mother-in-law (John and Donna), my brother and his wife (Nick and Holly), sister and her husband (Joëlle and Connor), my Uncle Bernard (a.k.a. "Dr. Plugger") and Aunt Joëlle, Cousin Shannon, Gisele and Lindsay Fee, Mark "It Was a Dark and Stormy Night" Zeleny and his wife Mary, and "The Twins" (Kathy and Niel), were a continual source of encouragement. And, of course, I would be remiss to leave out my daughters, Ava and Olivia, who always reminded me when it was time to put aside my work and play "dolls" on the carpet.

Lastly, I'd like to give a loving nod to my wife, Lisa. This project required many mornings at the library gathering research, many afternoons at the kitchen table transcribing notes, and many late nights in front of a laptop. Lisa was always armed with a patient smile and a willingness to reread chapters, no matter the hour. She is my biggest cheerleader, my best friend, and my rock.

About the Author

Chris Scarnati is a sportswriter and English teacher. He covered the New Orleans Saints for the *Houma Times* in Louisiana, and his work has appeared on *SI.com, ESPN.com, Maxim.com*, and in the *New Orleans Times-Picayune* and the *Pittsburgh Tribune-Review* newspapers. He has also been a regular guest on ESPN Radio.

Since graduating from the University of Missouri School of Journalism in 2000, Chris has captured numerous writing awards for his feature stories, personality profiles, and columns.

Chris resides in Valencia, Pennsylvania, with his wife and two daughters. *Fighting Till the End* is his first book.

Printed in Great Britain
by Amazon